# DISEASES DISORDERS

# Asperger's Syndrome

## Toney Allman

**LUCENT BOOKS**

*A part of Gale, Cengage Learning*

GALE
CENGAGE Learning

Detroit • New York • San Francisco • New Haven, Conn • Waterville, Maine • London

GALE
CENGAGE Learning™

**LIBRARY OF CONGRESS CATALOGING-IN-PUBLICATION DATA**

Allman, Toney.
  Asperger's syndrome / by Toney Allman.
    p. cm. — (Diseases & disorders)
  Includes bibliographical references and index.
  ISBN 978-1-4205-0111-7 (hardcover)
  1. Asperger's syndrome—Juvenile literature.  I. Title.
  RC553.A88A45 2009
  616.85'8832—dc22

                                                            2008042746

Lucent Books
27500 Drake Rd.
Farmington Hills, MI 48331


ISBN-13: 978-1-4205-0111-7
ISBN-10: 1-4205-0111-9

Printed in the United States of America
1 2 3 4 5 6 7 13 12 11 10 09

# Table of Contents

# "The Most Difficult Puzzles Ever Devised"

**C**harles Best, one of the pioneers in the search for a cure for diabetes, once explained what it is about medical research that intrigued him so. "It's not just the gratification of knowing one is helping people," he confided, "although that probably is a more heroic and selfless motivation. Those feelings may enter in, but truly, what I find best is the feeling of going toe to toe with nature, of trying to solve the most difficult puzzles ever devised. The answers are there somewhere, those keys that will solve the puzzle and make the patient well. But how will those keys be found?"

Since the dawn of civilization, nothing has so puzzled people— and often frightened them, as well—as the onset of illness in a body or mind that had seemed healthy before. A seizure, the in-ability of a heart to pump, the sudden deterioration of muscle tone in a small child—being unable to reverse such conditions or even to understand why they occur was unspeakably frustrating to healers. Even before there were names for such conditions, even before they were understood at all, each was a reminder of how complex the human body was, and how vulnerable.

4

While our grappling with understanding diseases has been frustrating at times, it has also provided some of humankind's most heroic accomplishments. Alexander Fleming's accidental discovery in 1928 of a mold that could be turned into penicillin has resulted in the saving of untold millions of lives. The isolation of the enzyme insulin has reversed what was once a death sentence for anyone with diabetes. There have been great strides in combating conditions for which there is not yet a cure, too. Medicines can help AIDS patients live longer, diagnostic tools such as mammography and ultrasounds can help doctors find tumors while they are treatable, and laser surgery techniques have made the most intricate, minute operations routine.

This "toe-to-toe" competition with diseases and disorders is even more remarkable when seen in a historical continuum. An astonishing amount of progress has been made in a very short time. Just two hundred years ago, the existence of germs as a cause of some diseases was unknown. In fact, it was less than 150 years ago that a British surgeon named Joseph Lister had difficulty persuading his fellow doctors that washing their hands before delivering a baby might increase the chances of a healthy delivery (especially if they had just attended to a diseased patient)!

Each book in Lucent's Diseases and Disorders series explores a disease or disorder and the knowledge that has been accumulated (or discarded) by doctors through the years. Each book also examines the tools used for pinpointing a diagnosis, as well as the various means that are used to treat or cure a disease. Finally, new ideas are presented—techniques or medicines that may be on the horizon.

Frustration and disappointment are still part of medicine, for not every disease or condition can be cured or prevented. But the limitations of knowledge are being pushed outward constantly; the "most difficult puzzles ever devised" are finding challengers every day.

# Strangers in a Foreign Land

Asperger's syndrome is a mild form of autism that causes problems with everyday socialization, communication, and relating to other people. It is a confusing combination of abilities and disabilities, strengths and weaknesses, talent and disorder. People with Asperger's have normal or high intelligence and yet struggle with understanding social rules, making friends, and grasping how to engage in casual conversations. They may be physically uncoordinated and immature and yet have extraordinary special talents and memorization skills. They may seem emotionally unresponsive and yet feel things very deeply. A person with Asperger's syndrome seems different and does not "fit in." He or she may be labeled a loner, an eccentric, a weirdo, a freak, or an uncool geek by classmates and peers. People with Asperger's syndrome often say that they feel as if they are foreigners in a strange country. They have a different way of thinking and find it hard to fathom the language, thinking processes, and culture of the natives who inhabit this foreign land.

Damian, an eighteen-year-old high school graduate with Asperger's syndrome, knows what that feeling is like, but he does not want to be defined by his Asperger's syndrome. He prefers to use his high intelligence and original thinking skills to concentrate on his passion for history and his gift for creative writing. In the ninth grade Damian won second place in a statewide short story contest sponsored by the Virginia High School League, and yet he had terrible problems learning to control a pencil so that he could write. He always read far above his grade level but struggled with frustration and concentration in the classroom. Damian is a loner and has problems with the social world, but he is comfortable with who he is. He says, "I often approach an idea or subject with a viewpoint that's different than many other people." And he is just fine with that different viewpoint. He focuses on his writing and his history research and enjoys solitary activities such as walking in the woods. He has written about being "fortunate enough to find a place in which to escape civilization, to find peace."[1]

Damian may not love going to parties or hanging out with the crowd, but he appreciates and is deeply sensitive to nature. He once wrote about a favorite pond:

> The way the trees on the far bank would toss their heads in the wind. Sometimes somewhere a bird or squirrel would break the stillness or a fish would make a faint splash by rising to the surface. Or maybe you would see a deer lower its muzzle into the water to drink; if spotted it would rise and flee, tail up, with great bounds. Most of the time though nothing but the whispering of the wind could be heard. This was where I came to watch and learn . . . and to fish.[2]

Damian likes stillness, quiet, and simplicity. He is one face of Asperger's syndrome, and there are many thousands more. All of them need to find a comfortable place for themselves in the world. They just need the help, support, acceptance, and understanding of their differences that will make that possible.

# CHAPTER ONE

# What Is Asperger's Syndrome?

**A**sperger's syndrome is a developmental disorder of childhood, meaning that it interrupts or delays the normal growth and acquisition of abilities as a person matures. It is also called Asperger's disorder, Asperger syndrome, or just AS. Psychiatrist Lorna Wing refers to it as a mysterious, puzzling, and fascinating disorder because it can be so difficult to identify and to understand. Nevertheless, AS is generally characterized by a basic triad of developmental problems. The delays and interruptions of AS occur in social and emotional interactions, language and communication skills, and in flexibility of thought and imagination. These disabilities exist despite normal and often gifted intellectual capabilities.

## Social and Emotional Problems

Normal social and emotional interactions are difficult for people with AS to understand. They may be happiest alone and have trouble making friends because they cannot read facial expressions or correctly interpret body language and gestures. Because of this, they may fail to empathize with the feelings of others. As typical children grow up, they learn almost automatically how to read an angry grimace, a puzzled frown, a welcoming smile, a sad, quivering mouth, and many other

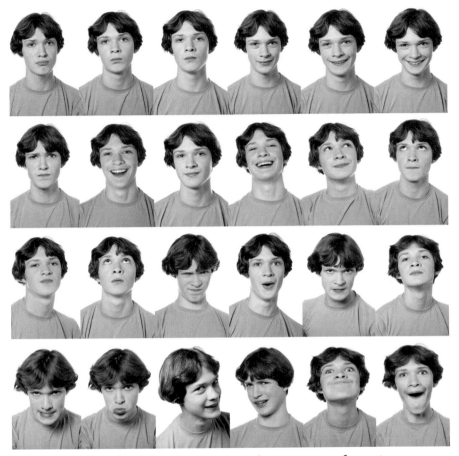

A series of one boy's facial expressions shows a range of emotion.
People with Asperger's syndrome are unable to correctly interpret
other people's facial expressions, gestures, and body language that
can reveal their feelings.

emotions that people express on their faces. People with AS
do not naturally know what these facial signals mean. They
have the same trouble with the body language that typical people read easily. They cannot interpret the tense body of an of-
fended or angry companion. They do not see the signals of
discomfort or boredom in crossed arms, backing up when
someone gets too close, or turning one's back on someone.
People with AS know they are missing cues or doing things
wrong; they just cannot understand why they are failing to

figure out other people. They may feel detached from the rest of the world and unable to change this isolation.

Asperger's syndrome also causes difficulties in expressing one's own emotions. Facial expressions and body language may not reflect feelings accurately. A person with AS may smile when he or she is told a sad story. His or her face may look rigid, expressionless, or robotic to other people. They may assume that the person with AS has no feelings. Eye contact can be a big problem for people with AS, too. Many AS people do not look others in the eye when they are listening or talking. Other people may assume this means disinterest, rudeness, dishonesty, or defiance, but for an AS person, eye contact may feel unnecessary or even uncomfortable.

## Language and Communication Problems

Verbal language is a critical form of social communication that is also impaired for people with AS. Children with AS develop normal language skills at the normal age. As they grow up, they often have high vocabularies and reading levels. However, their use of language can seem stilted and artificial. They may speak in a monotone, instead of with expression. They may sound like serious little adults. Even when they are teens or adults, people with AS can seem overly serious and may have problems with using language as others do. Joking, teasing, and social small talk may make no sense. Psychologist and AS expert Tony Attwood says, "I have the impression that many people with Asperger's syndrome consider a conversation to be primarily an opportunity to exchange information, to learn

or inform, and if there is no practical information to exchange, why waste time talking?"[3] This approach can result in the Asperger's individual interrupting others' conversations or talking on and on about a subject of interest even though the other person is bored and uninterested. Friends might interpret the behavior as rude or disrespectful, but a person with AS does not mean to be impolite. He or she just does not grasp the normal give-and-take of conversation. Temple Grandin, a grown woman with this difficulty, explains: "I have observed that when several people are together and having a good time, their speech and laughter follow a rhythm. . . . I have always had a hard time fitting in with this rhythm, and I usually interrupt conversations without realizing my mistake. The problem is that I can't follow the rhythm."[4]

People with Asperger's syndrome may have difficulty managing the exchange of normal conversation despite a good vocabulary and language skills.

A person with AS may also be confused by conversation that typical people assume is completely clear. An individual with Asperger's usually takes language literally and cannot understand idioms, implied requests, sarcasm, or figures of speech. For example, a mother may say to her AS child, "I'm losing patience with you," and the child may decide to help her look for it.[5] If someone says "How are you?" an older person with AS may not say "Fine," but instead begin a long monologue about his or her physical or mental state.

People with AS have both a problem with social skills and a problem with grasping how people typically use words to relate to each other. Attwood explains:

> An example of a relatively simple literal interpretation of what the other person says was when a young man was asked by his father to make a pot of tea. Some time later his father was concerned that he had not received his refreshment and asked his son, "Where's the tea?" His son replied, "In the pot, of course." His son was unaware that the original request implied not just the preparation of the tea, but the presentation of a cup of tea for each person. The person with Asperger's syndrome is not being deliberately lazy, obtuse [dense], or defiant, but responding to the literal, not the implied, meaning.[6]

Because people with Asperger's do not understand social language, they do not know how to respond to other people appropriately. They are very logical and often have trouble seeing the sense of using language in illogical, imprecise ways. They can consider the social rules of conversation tricky and confusing. People with AS can be like foreigners trying to grasp a brand new language and culture. The words and meaning in social conversation are grasped very slowly and with a lot of mistakes.

Some mistakes happen because it is so hard to generalize from one situation to the next. Just because a person learns to say "I'm fine" when greeted with "How are you?" does not mean he or she knows what to say when asked "What's up?" A lack of social imagination means it is hard to be flexible with

# Asperger's or Autism?

Actress Daryl Hannah was diagnosed as having "autistic tendencies" when she was three years old. She had few friends and daydreamed a lot in school. Today she says, "I maybe had Asperger's. It wasn't widely understood at the time." If she does have Asperger's syndrome or mild autism, she has overcome most of her childhood problems as an adult. However, she is still well-known for her shyness and her dislike of publicity. She is more comfortable acting a role than talking about her real life. She is so anxious about public appearances that she once had to take a tranquilizer to be able to attend an Oscar ceremony. She lives a very private life and rarely gives interviews. She is extremely passionate about ecology and living a lifestyle that does not harm the planet. Whether these characteristics are related to special interests, social interaction problems, and emotional confusions cannot be known for sure, but despite any disorder she may have, she has achieved success in living a normal life and functioning normally in society.

Quoted in John-Paul Flintoff, "Hollywood's Full-On Green Guerrilla," *Times Online*, December 2, 2007. http://women.timesonline.co.uk/tol/life_and_style/women/celebrity/article2982771.ece.

Actress Daryl Hannah, who was diagnosed as having "autistic tendencies" as a child, says she now considers the possibility that she has Asperger's syndrome.

social behavior. One AS individual explains, "We have trouble working out what other people know. We have more difficulty guessing what other people are thinking."[7] This lack of empathy does not mean that a person with AS lacks sympathy. He or she likely cares very much about other people's feelings. However, reading those feelings and putting oneself in another's shoes is often impossible.

## Flexibility and Imagination Problems

A lack of empathy can make a person with AS behave rigidly and believe that there is only one way to do things. Situations are right or wrong, black or white. It can be difficult to understand that other people may prefer a different way or feel different emotions. This problem with social imagination is the last leg of the AS triad. It means that children with AS may not be able to play pretend games, even though they are gifted in mathematics or well-versed in computer technology. It means they may dissolve in frustration when someone plays with a toy "in the wrong way."

This inflexibility can pervade other areas of life with AS. People may depend on a rigid routine in their daily lives and resist change. They prefer sameness and become upset and flustered if they have to move from classroom to classroom or eat breakfast before showering when they are used to the reverse. A need for sameness may, in an extreme, manifest itself in a fascination for watching the spinning wheels of a toy car rather than actually playing with the car. It may be evident in constant rocking motions to soothe and calm oneself or twiddling the fingers repetitively.

## Asperger's Syndrome Is an Autism Spectrum Disorder

Watching wheels spin, rocking the body, and twiddling are kinds of self-stimulation that are identified as autistic behaviors. Asperger's syndrome is considered by experts to be related to autism. Autism is a severe development disorder in which an infant may begin to develop normally but then regresses in ability. He or she stops responding to other people

A boy with autism plays with a toy at a shop while on a school field trip. Although the symptoms of autism tend to be more severe in comparison, Asperger's syndrome is considered one of a range of disorders on the autism spectrum.

# Autism Spectrum Disorders

Of the five developmental disorders included on the autism spectrum, autistic disorder symptoms are the most severe, while those of Asperger's are mildest.

## Symptoms

| | |
|---|---|
| **Autistic disorder** | Significant impairment in social interaction and communication; limited range of interests and activities; delay in language development |
| **Rett's disorder** | Rare condition similar to autistic disorder; affects only girls |
| **Asperger's syndrome** | A milder form of autism, but with no delay in language development |
| **Childhood disintegrative disorder** | Rare condition; children have early normal development, then suffer significant loss of previously acquired skills |
| **Pervasive developmental disorder** | Autistic children who do not fit into the other four disorder categories on the spectrum |

## Prevalence

- **Autism disorder is the most common of the 5 autism spectrum disorders, affecting an estimated 1 in 166 births.**

- **As many as 1.5 million Americans have some form of autism.**

- **Disorders occur 3 to 4 times more often in boys than in girls.**

- **Autism disorders are increasing at an estimated rate of 10–17 percent each year.**

- **Experts estimate that up to 4 million Americans could be affected by some form of autism over the next 10 years.**

Taken From: *Autism Spectrum Disorders* (*Pervasive Developmental Disorders* [Addendum]), Centers for Disease Control and Prevention, February 2007. (The CDC notes that its studies do not provide a national estimate.) www.nimh.nih.gov/. Pamla E. Brown, "What Is All This Talk About Autism & Asperger's Syndrome?" Symposium on Autism, Brazosport College, April 2008. www.brazosport.edu.

except in very limited ways. Any words are lost, and language abilities fail to develop. The child is unable to form loving and social relationships, resists being touched, seems uninterested in people, and has an intense need for sameness in the environment. Self-stimulation and repetitive movements are common. Usually the child's intelligence tests as subnormal or retarded. Some autistic people, however, can be highly intelligent, learn to speak and relate to others, and overcome many of their disabilities with training and therapy. When the disability is severe, most experts say that autistic people are lost and locked in their own little worlds. Many seem not to recognize that the world is out there, and they may require lifelong care.

Autism, however, is not a neat label that fits every individual with certain specific symptoms. That is because individuals may have so many different symptoms in varying degrees. Specialists are still learning how to recognize autistic disorders, how they affect people, and even what to name them. Arguments continue about which people are autistic and which are not, as well as which symptoms are most important. In recent years, experts have realized that autism can range from mild to severe and that people who are not truly autistic may evidence autistic traits.

Psychiatrists, psychologists, and educators now recognize that there is an autism spectrum—a range of autistic disorders. So far experts recognize five distinct developmental disorders on the spectrum. On this spectrum, people may range from nonverbal and unreachable to brilliant and gifted but a little "odd." Autism, of course, is one of the developmental disorders. Two other rare disorders are Rett's disorder (which is like autism except that it affects only girls) and childhood disintegrative disorder (in which a child develops normal language abilities and then loses them). The term for a person with autistic problems who does not fit into any other autistic categories is pervasive developmental disorder not otherwise specified. And finally, Asperger's syndrome is the disorder on the high-functioning end of the autistic spectrum, marked by normal language development and normal intelligence. Autism expert and clinical psychologist Uta Frith says that people with

AS have "a dash of autism";[8] others call it a mild form of autism. Those with AS have the same triad of social, emotional, and communication problems as autistics do, but these symptoms are not as severe or as limiting as they are in the other disorders on the spectrum.

People with AS may be on the high-functioning end of the spectrum, but that does not mean that they do not face significant difficulties in relating to the rest of the world. In addition there is a range of severity among AS individuals, from mild to serious, within the triad of impairments. Along with the social and language problems, people with AS also commonly experience and perceive the world in a different—sometimes autistic —way. Sometimes, these differences cause more problems for the individual as he or she tries to fit into society. Sometimes they can actually turn out to be advantages.

## Special Interests

Most people with AS have a special interest, or a preoccupation or fascination with a particular subject. With a young child, the special interest may be collecting batteries or learning all about vacuum cleaners. The interest may be so absorbing that the child has trouble focusing on anything else and spends many hours a day concentrating on and talking about the special interest. It may be obsessive, to the point where the person exhibits an excessive need to be involved in the special interest.

Special interests, however, can be positive aspects of AS. With their ability to concentrate intently and memorize facts and details about an interesting topic, people with AS can become extremely knowledgeable in the area of special interest. Since special interests change as children mature, special interests often become special talents. It may not be valuable to love AA batteries, but it can be very useful to know all there is to know about opera or how a computer works. Many AS people develop special talents and skills in mathematics, computer technology, music, or art and become experts in their fields when they are grown.

With normal or gifted intelligence, an extremely logical mind, and the ability to focus on a particular topic until it is completely

# Asperger's Savants

Perhaps 10 percent of people with an autism spectrum disorder are savants. A savant is a person with a developmental disability who has an area of brilliance or a remarkable talent. Although no one knows why, many more people with Asperger's syndrome are savants than are typical people. Some experts hypothesize that the extraordinary skill arises from the ability to concentrate and focus on a special interest. Some of the most common savant skills involve amazing memory capabilities, early musical genius, and performing complex mathematical calculations in one's head. Jerry Newport, for example, is a savant with Asperger's syndrome. Since he was seven years old, he could instantly solve multiplication problems involving huge numbers without pencil and paper. He can calculate square roots to many decimal places, announce in a moment what day of the week any date in history falls on, and tell strangers how many hours, minutes and seconds it has been since they were born when given their birth dates. Qazi Fazli Azeem, another Asperger's savant, can understand almost nothing mathematical, but he is a high-speed reader with a phenomenal memory and can remember entire books he has read. Many people with Asperger's syndrome have special talents, but few are actual savants.

understood, a person with AS is equipped with assets as well as impairments. However, he or she may need all these assets to overcome the problems associated with AS. Using logic and intelligence to figure out socially acceptable conversation is much harder than intuitively understanding how to have a friendly chat. Noting and memorizing what facial expressions mean is an arduous chore that may make a person with AS prefer to avoid people instead of trying to socialize. People with AS want friends, want to fit in, and want to be accepted. They are very aware that they don't fit into society. Yet the accepted rules of social behavior make no sense to them.

## Other Asperger's Syndrome Impairments

To make matters worse, AS is often accompanied by other problems. Many people with AS also have attention deficit/hyperactivity disorder (ADHD). They have trouble concentrating and trouble holding still. They may also have trouble with senses that are acutely responsive and overreactive. This is called hypersensitivity or sensory overload. It means that sounds, sights, smells, and touches that seem normal and unimportant to typical people may feel unbearable to people with AS. Noises may be screamingly loud; the touch of rough cloth may be painful; bright lights in the classroom may feel like an attack on the eyes that has to be shut out. Crowds of people may feel so confusing and overwhelming that an AS individual has to escape, rock, or twiddle to sooth himself or herself, or just melt down and fall apart.

Claire Sainsbury has Asperger's syndrome. She describes how difficult a school day can be for a person with this sensitivity:

A busy classroom, with its lights, noises, smells, and flurry of activity, can be difficult to bear for students with Asperger's syndrome, who tend to be highly sensitive to sensory stimulation.

The corridors and halls of almost any mainstream school are a constant tumult of noises echoing, fluorescent lights (a particular source of visual and auditory stress for people on the autistic spectrum), bells ringing, people bumping into each other, the smells of cleaning products and so on. For anyone with sensory hyper-sensitivities and processing problems typical of an autistic spectrum condition, the result is that we often spend most of our day perilously close to sensory overload.[9]

Sensory overload is but one barrier to school success. Many people with AS are also awkward. Their motor coordination is impaired, and so they may have tremendous difficulty with skills like holding a pencil or catching a ball. In small children this means a delay in developing motor skills such as running, skipping, coloring, cutting with scissors, or tying one's shoelaces. In older kids it means lack of success at team sports, illegible writing, or trouble balancing and coordinating body movements for dancing or driving a car.

## The Stress of Asperger's Syndrome

The difference between AS individuals and most others on the autism spectrum is that people with AS know something is wrong with them. They wonder why they are so different. And it hurts.

Because of their awareness, people with AS may develop emotional problems. They can become so anxious and frightened in social situations that they have panic attacks. They may become so angry and frustrated that they have tantrums or bouts of rage. They are at risk of developing real depression and even committing suicide. Emotional problems are worse for people who do not know why they have the trouble they do. Most people with AS are in this category. Their AS is not diagnosed until they are teenagers or adults. By this time, explains Michael John Carley, a man with AS, the "individual has been made to feel bad about what separates him or her from the rest of the world."[10] Unfortunately diagnosing AS can be quite difficult, especially when the symptoms are mild.

# CHAPTER TWO

# Diagnosing Asperger's Syndrome

**D**iagnosing someone with Asperger's syndrome is a subjective decision that depends on the knowledge and experience of the clinicians, or professionals, who are performing the examination and comparing the individual to other people with the disorder. It is as much art as science, because the cluster of symptoms can be so variable, because so many of the symptoms appear in other disorders or in normal individuals, and because recognition of AS is so new.

## Identifying a Syndrome

Asperger's syndrome was first described by an Austrian psychiatrist, Hans Asperger, in 1944. His description, however, received little attention until 1981, when British psychiatrist Lorna Wing rediscovered his paper and named the disorder Asperger's syndrome in his honor. She had observed children and adults very much like the ones Asperger described and suggested that these people displayed a special kind of autism that needed a name of its own. Her descriptions and conclusions interested other psychiatrists and psychologists, who began identifying the group of symptoms and behaviors in patients of their own. Finally, in 1994 Asperger's syndrome became an official psychiatric diagnosis in the United States.

Asperger's syndrome is a psychological and psychiatric diagnosis, but this does not mean that it is a mental illness, brain damage, "craziness," mental retardation, or emotional sickness. Rather, the diagnosis is one of learning differences, developmental problems, behavioral difficulties, and brains that seem to work in a way that is nontypical. Professionals arrive at the diagnosis by identifying behaviors that seem to fit the symptoms of AS.

No blood test, no brain scan, no medical or psychological examination of any kind can identify a person with Asperger's syndrome. There is no single characteristic that separates people

# Hans Asperger

Hans Asperger was practicing medicine during the time when Austria was part of Nazi Germany. His paper describing the disorder he discovered was published during the height of World War II, when much of Europe and America rejected anything that seemed to be a part of Nazi thought. That is probably why his findings were lost and ignored for so many years. Asperger, however, was a strong opponent of Nazism. He was particularly disturbed by Nazi eugenics laws. These laws were an effort to purify the human race and eradicate people who were "defective" or not of pure German blood. The Nazis attacked not only Jews but also people perceived to be handicapped, mentally ill, or retarded. They believed in killing any child born with a hereditary disease. Asperger was disgusted by these ideas and bravely argued publicly that education could overcome any possible genetic problems. He did his best to save the children who were patients at his clinic by insisting that unusual traits were not signs of weakness or defects. He said, "Not everything that steps out of line, and thus [is] 'abnormal', must necessarily be 'inferior'."

Quoted in Tony Attwood, *The Complete Guide to Asperger's Syndrome*. London and Philadelphia: Jessica Kingsley, 2007, p. 11.

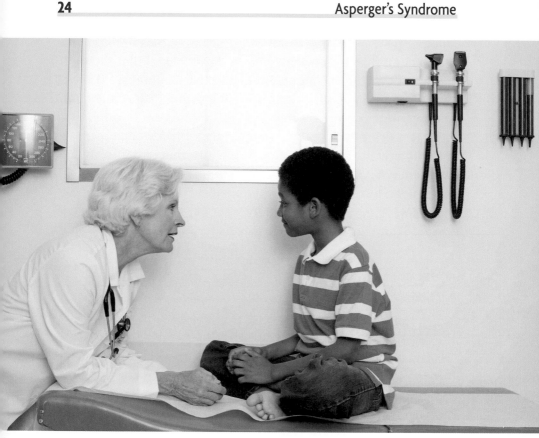

Asperger's syndrome is not something that can be diagnosed by a child's physician at a checkup. Instead, the opinions of a variety of professionals, including psychologists, teachers, speech therapists, and other specialists, are considered before a diagnosis is made.

with AS from normal people, autistic people, or people with other disorders. There is no one symptom or impairment that leads to a definite diagnosis of AS. Instead, professionals rely on interviews with the individual and with family members, psychological tests, reports from teachers, and their own previous experience with different psychological disorders to arrive at a diagnosis. They look for a whole constellation of behaviors that point to AS. Some of the characteristics and behaviors must be in evidence to diagnose Asperger's, but none of them prove a person has AS. Clinicians have to use their best judgment to diagnose the condition. And because the diagnosis of AS is so new, few people are skilled at recognizing it. Tony Attwood is an Australian psychologist considered to be one of the foremost experts on Asperger's syndrome today. He explains that the diagnostic process is like a "100-piece jigsaw puzzle." He says:

> Some pieces of the puzzle (or characteristics of Asperger's syndrome) are essential, the corner and edge pieces. When more than 80 pieces are connected, the puzzle is solved and the diagnosis confirmed. None of the characteristics are unique to Asperger's syndrome, however, and a typical child or adult may have perhaps 10 to 20 pieces or characteristics. . . . The ultimate decision on whether to confirm a diagnosis is based on the clinician's clinical experience, the current diagnostic criteria, and the effect of the unusual profile of abilities on the person's quality of life.[11]

## DSM-IV Criteria

Diagnostic criteria are standards for labeling someone with a disorder. In the United States these criteria are established by the American Psychiatric Association and published in the *Diagnostic and Statistical Manual of Mental Disorders* (*DSM-IV*). (*Mental* means psychological and related to thoughts and feelings, not "crazy.") Every psychiatrist and psychologist uses the *DSM-IV* criteria to make a diagnosis, because the standards are agreed to be the best tools so far available for recognizing and naming disorders.

*DSM-IV* classifies Asperger's syndrome as an autism spectrum disorder. It lists six areas of disability or behaviors that should be present to justify a diagnosis of AS:

A. Qualitative impairment in social interaction, as manifested by at least two of the following:

  1. marked impairments in the use of multiple nonverbal behaviors such as eye-to-eye gaze, facial expression, body postures, and gestures to regulate social interaction

  2. failure to develop peer relationships appropriate to developmental level [for example, a six-year-old may

not play with other children, but play beside them only, which is more normal for a two-year-old.]

3. a lack of spontaneous seeking to share enjoyment, interests, or achievements with other people (e.g., by a lack of showing, bringing, or pointing out objects of interest to other people)

4. lack of social or emotional reciprocity [give-and-take]

B. Restricted repetitive and stereotyped patterns of behavior, interests, and activities, as manifested by at least one of the following:

1. encompassing preoccupation with one or more stereotyped and restricted patterns of interest that is abnormal either in intensity or focus

2. apparently inflexible adherence [clinging] to specific, nonfunctional routines or rituals

3. stereotyped and repetitive motor mannerisms (e.g., hand or finger flapping or twisting, or complex whole-body movements)

4. persistent preoccupation with parts of objects [for example, interest in the wheels of toy cars or the parts of vacuum cleaners]

C. The disturbance causes clinically significant impairment in social, occupational, or other important areas of functioning

D. There is no clinically significant general delay in language (e.g., single words used by age 2 years, communicative phrases used by age 3 years)

E. There is no clinically significant delay in cognitive development [intelligence and learning ability] or in the development of age-appropriate self-help skills, adaptive behavior (other than social interaction), and curiosity about the environment in childhood

F. Criteria are not met for another specific Pervasive Developmental Disorder or Schizophrenia [a mental illness][12]

## Working Toward the Diagnosis

In other countries the criteria for diagnosing AS include some different standards (some include motor clumsiness, for example), but in the United States clinicians test for the criteria listed in *DSM-IV* if they suspect an individual may have AS. Usually a team of several professionals is involved before a diagnosis is made.

A young boy is tested on his responses to different facial expressions displayed on a computer screen. A variety of tests is used to determine whether a diagnosis along the autism spectrum, including Asperger's syndrome, is appropriate.

The psychiatrist, psychologist, or medical doctor, for example, may interview the individual and look for appropriate eye contact, conversational skills, and typical body language. A psychologist will administer an intelligence test. A speech therapist may test language ability. An occupational therapist checks fine motor skills (skills with small muscles such as in the fingers), as well as self-help skills like dressing oneself or tying shoelaces. A neurologist, a medical doctor specializing in the brain and nervous system, may need to rule out any signs that the individual has other brain disorders and may test for motor clumsiness and awkwardness. An educational specialist may administer tests to see if academic knowledge is age-appropriate.

If the individual is a child, parents will be asked about what age the child spoke his or her first word, spoke in sentences, learned to crawl, and other developmental milestones. If the individual is an adult, he or she might be requested to ask family members for these milestones. In general the evaluator is looking for evidence that the person developed as expected, since normal growth and development is one criterion for AS diagnosis.

Clinicians also perform some tests for empathy, the ability to imagine the thoughts of other people. In this area AS people test as not typical. One test involves a kind of game with dolls. It can be used with anyone suspected of having AS, whether they are children, teens, or adults. First the clinician shows the person two dolls that are named Sally and Anne. As the person watches, Sally is made to put a marble in a basket. Then the clinician takes her out of the room and shuts the door. Next the doll named Anne takes the marble out of the basket and hides it in a box. Now Sally is "allowed" to return to the room. The clinician asks the individual where Sally will look for the marble. Typical people, no matter what their age, say that Sally will look in the basket, because that was the last place she saw it before she left the room. A person with AS, however, might say that Sally will look in the box. A person with AS lacks the empathy to imagine that Sally's experiences are not his or her experiences. Sally did not "see" the marble being moved, even though the person being tested did. Psychiatrist James Robert Brasic explains: "Affected children, adolescents, and adults re-

# The Wrong Diagnosis

Asperger's syndrome is often misdiagnosed by professionals who have little experience with the syndrome. In one survey 67 percent of children eventually diagnosed with AS had been diagnosed with another disorder first. About 13 percent of them had received three different diagnoses before being seen by an AS expert. Children are commonly labeled as learning disabled, emotionally disturbed, or mentally ill before the diagnosis of AS is made.

peatedly incorrectly think that Sally will know the location of the marble because they do. Affected individuals do not recognize that Sally's understanding of the placement of the marble is different from theirs because she was absent when it was moved."[13] This kind of mistake happens even in people with superior intelligence because they have such a hard time putting themselves in another person's shoes. It is one of many clinical clues that a diagnosis of AS is justified.

Questions, observations, and tests with dolls are all part of the way that professionals reach a diagnosis of AS, but drawing conclusions from all these methods depends on the skill of the clinician. Different clinicians may interpret the same behaviors in different ways. For example, one professional may believe a person has AS because his or her language skills are normal, but another clinician may diagnose the person with autism because the person was slow to say his or her first words as a baby. Another might believe the person is mentally slow or has trouble following directions because he or she did not understand that Sally could not find the marble.

## Aiming for a Standard in Diagnosis

In order to make the diagnosis less subjective and more standardized, some experts have developed questionnaires and interviews that can be scored. In these tests the clinician either answers questions or asks the person being tested or the family to answer questions. Points are assigned according to the way the questions are answered. The points are added up, and a kind of Asperger's score is assigned when the total equals more than a certain number.

In Sweden leading AS expert Christopher Gillberg developed such a standard test in 2001. It is called the Asperger Syndrome Diagnostic Interview (ASDI). The interview is designed to be conducted with a close family member and then scored by the clinician. A family member is chosen, even when the person being diagnosed is an adult, because people with AS often do not recognize the unusual ways they relate to the world. Parents or brothers and sisters usually give more accurate information. The interview consists of twenty questions that cover not only the *DSM-IV* criteria but also Gillberg's Asperger criteria and the original criteria of Hans Asperger himself. Each question is scored either 1 or 0, for exhibiting the behavior or for its not being present. The ASDI includes twenty questions. Here is a sampling of questions from the interview:

- Does he/she exhibit considerable difficulties interacting with peers? If so, in what way?

- Is there a pattern of interest or a specific interest which takes up so much of his/her time that time for other activities is clearly restricted? If there is, please comment.

- Are there comprehension problems (including misinterpretations of literal/implied meanings)? If so, what kind of problems?

- Is his/her gaze stiff, strange, peculiar, abnormal or odd? If so, please characterize.

- Does he/she make limited use of gestures? If so, please comment.[14]

## Only a Tool

Most professionals believe that interviews and questionnaires such as the ASDI are valuable tools for diagnosing AS, but no

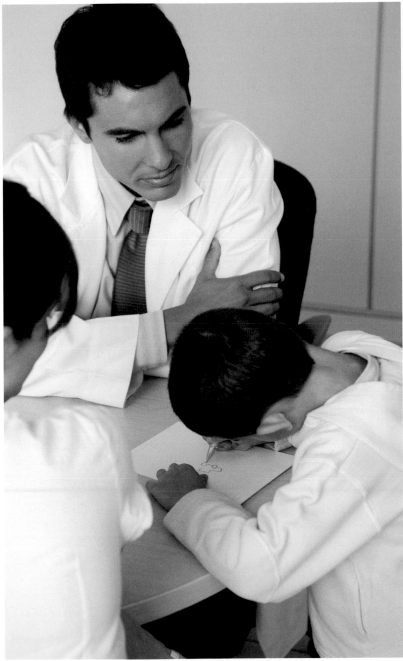

Clinicians who administer the variety of tests for Asperger's syndrome agree that no single tool is consistently reliable or valid in achieving a diagnosis.

A speech therapist works with a young child who has been diagnosed with autism. Some professionals argue that people diagnosed with Asperger's syndrome simply have a high-functioning form of autism or perhaps other conditions altogether.

one uses a single test all by itself as proof that a person has AS. The questions themselves are still subjective, and the total score still depends on the professional's judgment. None of the tests are 100 percent reliable. (Reliability is a measure of whether the same score can be obtained for the same person either by different clinicians administering the test for the same person or by the same interviewer giving the test multiple times for the same person.) The ASDI, for instance, is reliable most of the time, but not all the time for every person tested.

Validity is another measure of a test's usefulness. It is a measure of a test's accuracy and answers the question of whether the test correctly identifies people with AS and never indicates that someone has AS when he or she does not. Validity for most questionnaires and tests is measured by comparing results to professional diagnoses. So far there is no other measure of validity available. The ASDI is considered valid most of the time, but it can misclassify people as AS or miss someone who is already diagnosed as having the disorder. No AS test is 100 percent valid. Even Gillberg himself warns that the ASDI cannot distinguish between someone with AS and someone with high-functioning autism. Attwood asserts, "There is currently no convincing argument or data that unequivocally confirm that High Functioning Autism and Asperger's syndrome are separate and distinct disorders."[15]

## Asperger Controversy

Because a completely reliable and valid test for AS does not exist, some professionals wonder whether Asperger's is a real syndrome at all. They argue that not only is AS indistinguishable from high-functioning autism, but sometimes people may just have learning disabilities, ADHD, or psychiatric disorders. Some people are perhaps just odd, unfriendly loners, not individuals with a syndrome.

In 1998 Lorna Wing wrote, "Asperger syndrome and high-functioning autism are not distinct conditions." Psychiatrist Susan Dickerson Mayes and her colleagues agree with this statement. In 2001 they studied 157 children between the ages of five and fourteen who had been previously diagnosed with an autism spectrum disorder. The team was specifically interested in whether *DSM-IV* criteria for autism and AS could distinguish among the children and reveal differences in their behaviors. Mayes concluded that there were no valid reasons for diagnosing AS instead of autism. She and her team say:

> Children with autism who have relatively mild symptoms and high IQs are variously referred to by different clinicians as having autism, high-functioning autism, mild autism, Asperger's disorder or syndrome, pervasive developmental disorder not otherwise specified, or autistic features. This causes much confusion . . . [and] certainly has not been proven empirically.[16]

Mayes did add, however, that her study might have yielded different results if she had looked at older teens and adults. She was not sure if her conclusions applied only to younger children because they are harder to diagnose. Attwood also says that Asperger's cannot be reliably diagnosed in very young children.

## How Many People Merit a Diagnosis?

Despite the controversy about how to diagnose AS, most professionals and AS experts continue to believe it is a real disorder that can be distinguished from other disorders on the autism spectrum. Since it was first recognized, more and more people have been diagnosed with AS, as well as with other autism spectrum disorders. Many professionals argue that the increase in diagnosis is due to an improved awareness and the ability to identify people with the milder autistic traits. Others say that both autism and AS are overdiagnosed. They suggest that "quirky" or nonconforming children are being labeled unfairly.

Studies of the incidence of autistic spectrum disorders do point to a rising rate in populations. No one knows why this should be so, but both autism and AS seem to be more common now than they were in the past. In the United States, for example, 5,200 students were diagnosed with autism in 1991.

A boy attends class at Orion Academy, a high school in Moraga, California, for students with Asperger's syndrome and high-functioning autism. Since the early 1990s, the number of students diagnosed with conditions along the autism spectrum in the United States has skyrocketed.

By 2005 that number had risen to more than 192,000. By 2006 the prevalence of autism spectrum disorders was estimated to be 1 out of 166. These statistics might support the idea that both autism and AS are overdiagnosed, but most experts disagree. They point out that it was not until the 1990s that professionals began to recognize milder forms of autism. They remind the doubters that AS was not even a diagnosis until 1994. They explain that as the definition of autistic disorders broadened and changed to include milder autistic traits, it was natural that more people would be diagnosed.

As a matter of fact, many clinicians believe that AS is underdiagnosed. Attwood explains: "It is my clinical opinion that we are currently detecting and diagnosing about 50 percent of children who have Asperger's syndrome. Those who are not referred for a diagnostic assessment of Asperger's syndrome are able to camouflage their difficulties and avoid detection, or a clinician fails to see Asperger's syndrome and focuses on another diagnosis."[17] He estimates that the prevalence of AS is about 1 in 250 children. Since almost all of today's older teens and adults with Asperger's were not identified as having the disorder as children (because the diagnosis is so new), no one is sure about the prevalence in the total population. AutismHelp.org, a general information Web site about autism and related disorders, suggests that as many as 1.5 million Americans may have an autism spectrum disorder.

Whether or not AS is clearly defined, increasing in prevalence, or always diagnosed accurately, the experts continue to search for a better understanding of what AS is and why it happens in the first place.

# CHAPTER THREE

# Born Different: What Causes Asperger's Syndrome?

**A**sperger's syndrome seems to have a neurological cause. There is a problem with certain structures and systems in the brain such that AS brains do not operate in the same way that neurologically typical (neurotypical) brains do. This is not necessarily a malfunction, and it is not a disease or the result of bad childhood experiences. Tony Attwood explains, "In short, the brain is 'wired' differently, not necessarily defectively, and this was not caused by what a parent did or did not do during a child's development."[18] People with AS have brains that may cause them to think and respond differently than normal, neurotypical brains, but that does not mean that they are abnormal, wrong, or damaged. They are just different. Most experts believe that this different way of thinking and feeling is inborn, or present from birth, and is a result of genetic factors.

## Brain Works

Scientists have accumulated a good deal of neurological evidence about the brain differences that occur in AS in particular and in autism spectrum disorders in general. Today's medical technology allows researchers to watch living brains in action and find the areas of the brain where things seem to be wired differently.

# Autism and Vaccines

In the news and in popular opinion, there is a great fear that certain vaccines given routinely to babies could be the cause of autism. One vaccine that has come under suspicion is the measles, mumps, and rubella (MMR) vaccine. The theory is that the measles part of the vaccine causes a kind of inflammatory disease in the intestines of some children. This disease then spreads toxins to the brain that do damage and cause autism. Many parents today are afraid to allow their children to receive the MMR vaccine because they worry that it could cause autism. However, there is no medical proof that MMR vaccinations are dangerous. Because of public concern, researchers have instituted long-term studies to look for a connection between the MMR vaccine and autism. Although the evidence may change in the future, so far no studies have indicated that autism is brought on by vaccinations.

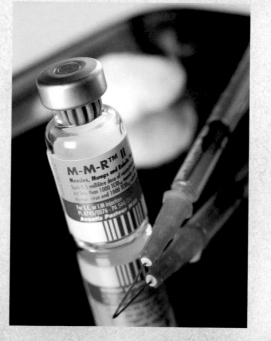

The MMR vaccine, given to babies in order to make children immune to the viruses that cause measles, mumps, and rubella, has been a target of concern for parents and some researchers who suspect a link between the vaccine and autism.

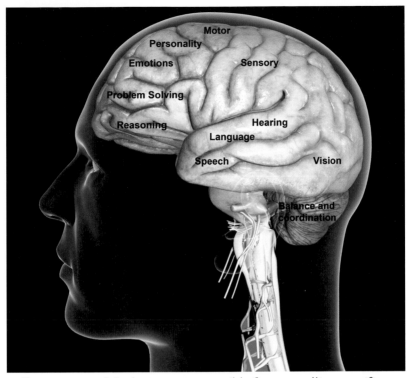

Different areas of the brain are responsible for controlling specific human functions, such as reasoning and problem solving, emotions, motor skills, language, and the senses.

Specific areas of the brain are responsible for controlling different functions and behaviors. The cerebral cortex is the area of the brain responsible for higher functions such as language, problem solving, thinking, emotions, reasoning, processing information, voluntary muscle control, and perceiving the environment. The cortex is a sheet of tissue, sometimes called gray matter, which is the outer layer of the brain.

The brain as a whole is divided down the middle into two equal halves called cerebral hemispheres. The hemispheres are each further divided into four lobes. They are the frontal lobes, the occipital lobes, the temporal lobes, and the parietal lobes. Scientists have identified and named the areas of the cortex and the lobes where specific functions occur. The frontal lobes are the parts at the very front of the brain. They are responsible for reasoning, speech, problem solving, and some emotional responses. The occipital lobes are at the back of the brain and are involved with vision. The parietal lobes are behind the frontal lobes and concerned with perception of pressure, pain, touch, and temperature. Below the frontal lobes are the temporal lobes. Here lies the amygdala, which seems to play an important role in emotions and feelings, as well as in memory. The amygdala is responsible for the fear that results in "fight or flight" responses and acts as the brain's emotional warning system.

## High-Tech Brain Scanning

Researchers can see inside people's brains and map all these structures using magnetic resonance imaging (MRI). With this technology they can compare the brain structures of typical people to people on the autistic spectrum and look for differences. An MRI is a medical test that uses a large magnet to create a magnetic field around a person's head. Then radio waves are sent through the magnetic field. A computer reads the wave signals and builds a detailed picture of the brain. Some MRI studies have shown that people with autism have differences in the frontal and parietal lobes of their brains when compared with neurotypical people. Other studies have suggested that the amygdala is smaller than normal and that its cells are smaller and more tightly packed than in typical brains.

In one study, a team of scientists led by psychiatrist Joseph Piven at the University of North Carolina compared the MRIs of thirty-eight people with autism with the MRIs of thirty-eight neurotypical people. The team discovered that almost half of the autistic people had larger brains than the people without autism. This larger size seemed to occur in certain regions of their brains, including in the frontal lobes.

Another study led by Dr. Antonio Y. Hardan at the University of Pittsburgh measured the thickness of the cortex in seventeen autistic boys and compared it with the thickness for fourteen normal boys. The cortices of the autistic boys were measurably thicker. Studies such as these suggest that true neurological differences are related to autism spectrum disorders, but no one knows yet why this is so. The differences do not show up 100 percent of the time, and scientists do not know how brain size is related to neurological dysfunction in autism. They do know, however, that evidence of brain differences shows up in almost all MRI studies of autistic people.

## Brains in Action

MRIs have also been used to identify activity in the brain as it is working or functioning. Even when areas of the brain look the same, scientists can identify the areas that function differently in autistic brains with a special kind of MRI called functional magnetic resonance imaging (fMRI). With fMRI, scientists can get an image of the blood flow in the area of the brain where activity is occurring. They can watch the brain as a person does specific tasks, such as solving math problems, looking at faces, or reading. They can see the changes in blood flow that indicate which part of the brain is being used to perform the tasks.

A researcher reviews a brain scan of a boy with autism to measure brain activity during a video game—like test. Studies of people with conditions along the autism spectrum show that brain activity differs from that of neurotypical people during certain tasks and situations.

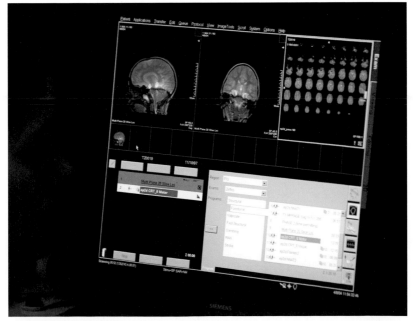

They can see how active that part of the brain becomes when it is required to perform those tasks. Some studies have found less activity in the frontal lobes of children with AS when they are asked to make judgments about social situations. Others have discovered that different areas of the brain are more active when people with AS are viewing images of facial expressions than the areas used by neurotypical people.

## A Brain Test

Mirella Dapretto, a psychiatrist at the University of California at Los Angeles, studied the social skills of eighteen boys with autistic spectrum disorders using fMRIs. She had them watch short cartoons of people having conversations. The boys were asked to figure out if the cartoon people were speaking sincerely or sarcastically. She compared the fMRIs with those of eighteen neurotypical boys who also watched the cartoons. The boys with autistic spectrum disorders showed less activity than normal in the frontal areas of the brain. Then she instructed all the boys to pay particular attention to the facial expressions and the tones of voice of the cartoon characters. The normal boys showed no change in brain activity. They already were concentrating on faces and tones of voice. The autistic spectrum disorder boys, however, responded to the instructions. They showed increases in brain activity as they did what other kids do naturally—notice the social cues.

Explains Dapretto: "The typically developing kids recognized and interpreted these cues automatically when trying to infer if a speaker's remark was sincere or sarcastic, so their brains were already responding appropriately. But not so with the ASD [autistic spectrum disorder] kids, who did not show activity in this area when specific instructions weren't provided." The fMRI results provided evidence that the boys were not defective, according to Dapretto. She says that "the fact that you can 'normalize' activity . . . clearly indicates there's nothing intrinsically wrong with this region in the autistic brain."[19] They could respond to social cues if they were told to do so; they just did not do it naturally.

# Too Many Males

About four times more boys than girls are diagnosed with autism spectrum disorders. Decades ago, autism expert Bernard Rimland pointed out that boys are just more likely to have hereditary diseases and organic damage than girls do. In this sense they are biologically weaker than girls are. Rimland's statement has been verified many times, but no one knows why it is the case. One theory involves the chromosomes that determine sex. They are called the X and Y chromosomes. Girls have two X chromosomes. Boys have an X and a Y. Many genetic traits are sex linked. This means that genes that cause defects can be on the X chromosome. (Genes for traits are very rare on Y chromosomes.) A girl, with two X chromosomes, may be protected from disease if one X chromosome has defects but the other is normal. A boy, because he has only one X chromosome, would be likely to have the disorder because his Y chromosome cannot protect him. It acts like a blank. As yet, however, no proof of genes for autism spectrum disorders on the X chromosome has been discovered.

Another theory is a social one. It suggests that girls with AS are just better at hiding their symptom than boys, so they are underdiagnosed. Perhaps they are better at imitating social skills and faking normalcy. Also, in American culture, it is more acceptable for girls to be shy, bad at sports, or to daydream. Their symptoms are not troublesome, and so they may not be referred for diagnosis by teachers and parents. Experts who argue for this theory say that AS probably really affects boys and girls equally.

## Human Social Brains

Psychiatrists have a theory about why people with autistic spectrum disorders do not automatically respond to social cues. They say that several regions and systems of the brain, particularly in the frontal and temporal areas of the cortex, work together to make up what they call the "social brain."

People with Asperger's syndrome may lack the ability to express empathy because they do not naturally recognize and understand the physical and verbal cues other people use to express emotion.

Some studies suggest that the amygdala is part of the functioning of the social brain, too. An organization named the Research Committee of the Group for the Advancement of Psychiatry explains, "The social brain is defined by its function—namely, the brain is a body organ that mediates [works out and makes connections about] social interactions while also serving as the repository [memory bank] of those interactions."[20] It is the social brain that most researchers believe is dysfunctional in people with AS, because of a difference in wiring.

According to psychological thought, because of the social brain, typical people develop a skill called theory of mind. Attwood explains that this "means the ability to recognize and understand thoughts, beliefs, desires and intentions of other people in order to make sense of their behaviour and predict what they are going to do next." Experts believe that people with AS do not have an adequate theory of mind. They are lacking empathy, or the ability to put themselves in someone else's shoes. Psychiatrists also call this ability "mind reading" and describe the inability to mind read as "mind blindness."[21]

Most typical people develop the ability to mind read accurately by the time they are five years old. People with AS, however, are often mind blind to some degree throughout their lives. Their theory of mind is immature or impaired, and they may even have trouble identifying and expressing their own emotions and feelings because of their mind blindness. Brain studies of adults with AS who are asked to watch social stories show less activity than normal in the areas of their brains that control theory of mind abilities. Instead of focusing on the social and emotional aspects of the stories, the brains with AS are apparently wired to pay attention to the physical, logical descriptions of what they see. They intellectually analyze situations, rather than responding with empathy to the feelings of story characters.

Neurotypical people mind read easily, without thought, and seemingly intuitively. They do this by watching facial expressions, looking into someone's eyes, listening to tones of voice, interpreting words and phrases of others, observing body language, and following the social cues that others give them. People with AS do not have the social capacity to do any of this easily. This does not mean their brains are defective and unable to respond to others at all. It does not mean they do not care about other people. As Attwood says, "The [AS] person does care, very deeply, but may not be able to recognize the more subtle signals of emotional states or 'read' complex mental states."[22]

## Mind Blindness and Genes

Understanding the neurological factors that lead to deficient theory of mind skills in people with AS is important. But knowing the effects of social brain impairments does not explain how the brains came to be wired in a different way. Most researchers and experts believe that AS has a genetic cause.

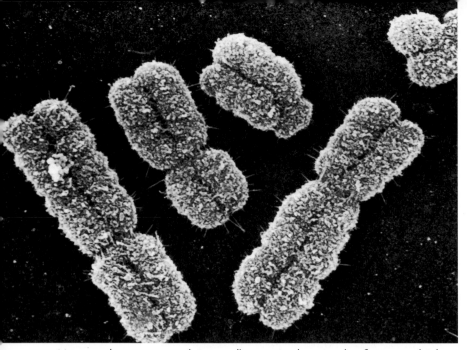

Human chromosomes (pictured) contain thousands of genes, which researchers are studying to determine variations that result in Asperger's syndrome and other autism spectrum disorders.

Genes are the basic units of inheritance for all living things. They are found inside the nucleus of almost every cell in the body. Genes are basically strings of deoxyribonucleic acid (DNA) that write the giant chemical book of instructions that codes for how a living being develops and functions. In human beings genes are arranged into twenty-three pairs of chromosomes. Each chromosome is made up of thousands of genes. Genes code for being a human, a mouse, or a daisy. They carry the coded instructions that tell heart cells to beat, eye cells to gather light, and brain cells to gather information. It is helpful to think of chromosomes as recipes and each gene as an ingredient. The instructions for the ingredients are spelled out by the DNA code.

Most genes and DNA are the same for all human beings, but some genetic instructions are unique to each individual. That is why people look different and have different natural abilities. It is also why some people have inherited disorders. Genes are inherited from one's parents, and each new individual receives half his or her genes from one parent and half from the other. Sometimes these genes carry slight changes, variations, or mistakes that occur when the DNA is being copied as the cells divide and new life develops. Such "typographical errors" can be passed on to the next generation, resulting in inherited diseases, or just causing differences in the way that an individual develops. Scientists believe this is the kind of process that results in AS and in autism spectrum disorders. But they do not believe that just one variant gene is responsible. They suspect that multiple genetic variations cause the neurological differences seen in AS. Finding these genes and understanding how they vary is an extremely complex task.

## Genetic Evidence and Autism Spectrum Disorders

Researchers do have evidence that AS runs in families. In one study, it was found that about 20 percent of fathers and 5 percent of mothers have symptoms of AS when they have a child diagnosed with AS. Brothers and sisters of a person with autism are 2 to 8 percent more likely to have an autism spectrum disorder than are people without a relative with autism. When all extended family members are examined (uncles, grandparents, cousins, and so on), more than 66 percent show some autistic symptoms and characteristics. For instance, relatives may have mild language problems, be loners, or have trouble empathizing with others.

Canadian researcher Peter Szatmari is one of the world's leading experts in the genetics of autism. He is a director of the worldwide Autism Genome Project. He and his team are looking for the specific chromosome where genes for autism spectrum disorders might be found. Szatmari's team has taken DNA samples from six thousand family members in which at least one person has an autism spectrum disorder. They use a kind of DNA fingerprinting to map the genes in each individual sample and to compare the DNA variations in a search for the genetic causes of spectrum disorders. So far the Autism Genome Project has identified a chromosome named chromosome 7 as an area of particular interest, as well as DNA variations on chromosome 2 and on chromosome 11. Szatmari has said, "Not only have we found *which* haystack the needle is in, we now know *where* in the haystack that needle is located." He says there are at least ten to twenty genes involved in autism, and he thinks that perhaps different combinations of these gene variations may be why some people have AS and others have different forms of autism. He explains about the research so far that "these findings not only tell us which chromosomes (or haystacks if you will) are involved, but where on the chromosome (or in the haystack) the genes might be."[23] As yet, however, neither Szatmari nor any other researcher has been able to identify for sure the specific genes involved in any of the autism spectrum disorders.

## Continuing the Search

Researchers such as Szatmari keep working on the genetics of autism and AS because they believe that a breakthrough will come in the near future and they will be able to identify the genes that cause the disorders. When that happens, firm diagnosis of autism spectrum disorders will be possible in even young infants. And that ability will make early treatment possible so that people with autism and AS can live happier, more comfortable lives.

Szatmari, along with most other scientists, does not believe that genetic causes mean that nothing can be done to change the ways that AS brains think and respond to the world. Since AS is a developmental disorder, over time, people can slowly improve their ability to form a theory of mind and to understand the ways in which neurotypical people relate to each other. They can use their logic and intellectual abilities to figure out emotions and empathy. Although there is no cure for AS, treatment and therapy can help people to make progress in their journey toward functioning in the neurotypical world. Attwood explains that many teens and adults with AS reach "a point on the continuum where only subtle differences and difficulties remain."[24] Most people with AS do not want to give up all their differences anyway, and many experts agree that they should not. They recognize that the AS way of thinking can be valuable and positive, but people with AS may need help with "getting" the rules under which much of society operates.

# CHAPTER FOUR

# Treatments and Therapies for Asperger's Syndrome

**A**sperger's has been called "wrong planet syndrome" because people with AS feel like aliens living in a strange world. There is no cure for being born on the wrong planet. There is no AS home planet to which they can return. They must learn to make sense of and fit into this neurotypical world. People with AS have the intellectual and logical skills to adapt to foreign ways of thinking, especially if other people make the effort to understand their theory of mind confusions and help them learn to function in this alien place. Many treatments and therapies have been developed to do just that—teach AS brains what neurotypical brains understand intuitively. The kind of therapy depends on the age of the person with AS and what kinds of problems he or she has in relating to others. Since many people with AS are not diagnosed until they are teenagers or adults, treatments and support are tailored to individual needs.

## Learning to Read Emotions

Cognitive behavioral therapy is one successful method of helping people with AS to develop a theory of mind by using their cognitive, or thinking, skills. Clinicians use cognitive behavioral therapy to help clients become aware of the emotions of

People with Asperger's syndrome can be taught to recognize the emotions behind someone's facial expression—for example, that someone who is smiling is likely expressing happiness.

others and their own emotions. The goals are to learn to recognize those emotions, to figure out how to express and control one's own emotions, and to use thinking skills to learn to handle emotions in real life.

One by one, the therapist and person with AS explore different emotions. First they explore a positive emotion, such as happiness. They may make an emotional scrapbook that has pictures, drawings, and photographs that illustrate happiness. Since people with AS have trouble understanding what makes other people happy if it does not make them happy, the scrapbook is about something that gives the AS person pleasure. If the individual is a very young child, the scrapbook may have pictures of smiling or laughing people. It may have pictures of people doing happy things, such as opening presents or riding a merry-go-round or playing a game. For older people the scrapbook will include pictures of the things that person enjoys most. For example, if a person with AS has a special interest in reptiles, the scrapbook can include many pictures of different reptiles and of scientists studying reptiles.

This scrapbook exercise helps people with AS to label the emotion of happiness correctly, but it can do much more. One person's scrapbook can be compared with the scrapbooks of other AS people. Everyone can compare scrapbooks and notice that different things make different people happy. Then everyone can talk about putting oneself in someone else's shoes. They can intellectually understand that people are made happy by different experiences. Eventually people with AS can learn to cheer up someone else or relate to another person's interests by recognizing what makes other people happy.

The scrapbooks can also be used to learn to recognize and label emotional cues. People can make a list of the thoughts, body sensations, and facial expressions that go along with being happy. After they have learned to recognize their own emotion, they can learn to recognize the same emotion in others. They can study facial expressions in pictures and learn to label happiness in other people. Experts believe that this education is actually training the amygdala in the brain to send chemical signals to the frontal lobes about a person's correct emotional state. Once a person can read his or her own emotional state correctly, it becomes possible to develop a theory of mind about others' emotions, too.

Scrapbooks are made about negative emotions, too, such as anger, fear, frustration, and sadness. People learn about the science of fear and anger, for example. They learn how these emotions increase heart rate, cause sweating, make muscles tense up, and make it harder to think clearly. When they can recognize and name the emotions in themselves, they can practice reading these emotions in others. One activity that helps is called "guess the message."[25] Perhaps the scrapbook includes photographs of the person's family members showing different emotions on their faces. The person looks at the faces and tries to read the proper emotion by intellectually noticing the signals explained by the therapist—wrinkled foreheads, big grins, or glaring eyes. With practice, this exercise becomes easier, and so does understanding facial expressions.

## Hundreds of Emotions to Memorize

Of course, humans display a wide range of emotions, often with very subtle changes in expression, tone of voice, and body language. There is a difference, for example, between rage and mild irritation, as well as a large range of feelings between the two extremes. Over time and with maturity, people with AS can become adept at understanding all the emotions that neurotypical people intuitively display and feel. They are learning the mind reading that comes naturally to neurotypical people.

Simon Baron-Cohen, a clinical psychologist at Oxford University in England, led a scientific team that identified 412 human emotions and then developed a computer program named Mind Reading: The Interactive Guide to Emotions. It is a tool for people with autism spectrum disorders that lets them watch short stories of six different actors responding to 412 situations with appropriate emotions. One of the actors in the program is Daniel Radcliffe, the actor who plays Harry Potter in films. One of the emotions he demonstrates is the kind of disgust a person might feel when given a raw squid to eat. The whole interactive program teaches theory of mind skills with videos, definitions, exercises, and quizzes that are fun and can be used alone or with a teacher. Users can choose one actor and change the expression of emotions to watch the way his or her face changes from happy to sad or from friendly to angry. In a 2006 study, Baron-Cohen and his colleague Ofer Golan tested the benefits of the Mind Reading program with adults with AS. They concluded, "Using *Mind Reading* for a relatively short period of time [ten weeks] allows users to learn to recognize a variety of complex emotions and mental states."[26]

Young people with Asperger's syndrome participate in a program that uses a theater setting to help them develop social skills.

## Dealing with Social Language

Language problems are also directly related to theory of mind skills, because people use words to express emotions in ways that are often puzzling to literal-minded people with AS. Carol Gray, an educator and expert in autism spectrum disorders, has created treatment techniques that teach social information and appropriate behaviors. Her methods teach in a way that makes sense to AS people who have trouble understanding what other people are thinking when they use words and phrases that imply larger or different meanings. Gray's Social Stories™ are a way to explain the thoughts, feelings, and behaviors of neurotypical people. Using the Social Stories™ kit, short stories are written by a therapist, teacher, or parent with the help of the individual with AS, following the pattern that Gray developed.

Gray says that the goal of the stories is "to seek to understand the student's perspective, to ensure a student has the social information he/she needs, and to present information so it is accessible and easily understood. As a result, every social story has a reassuring, accepting quality—positively and matter of factly describing a specific event."[27] Each Social Story™ is written to help an AS individual deal with a social situation that is a problem for him or her. For example, a person with AS may not understand that it is considered impolite to interrupt when two other people are talking. A Social Story™ could be written that explains and defines what interrupting means. It might then tell what the people could be thinking when they are interrupted. The story could end with what "I" do when I want to talk but do not want to interrupt.

Another teaching tool developed by Gray is called Comic Strip Conversations. These are short comic strips, peopled by two or more stick figures, that illustrate a social situation. Balloons connected to each figure's mouth show what the people are saying. Wavy, cloudlike balloons show what a person could be thinking. This tool also teaches about specific social situations in which a person with AS might feel confused. For instance, a person with AS may not recognize when someone is offering friendship. Instead of saying "I want to be your friend" (which is literal and specific), the other person might say "I bet I can beat you at chess." Neurotypical people would, assuming the tone is friendly, interpret the statement as an invitation to a chess match. A person with AS, however, might think he or she is being insulted. He or she might think the speaker is making a statement of fact that requires no response. A trained teacher or clinician could put this situation into a Comic Strip Conversation that explained the friendliness that is implied. Different speech and thinking balloons would show what the speaker might have meant. Thinking and speech balloons for the other stick figure might describe a thought of, "That is friendly and sounds fun," and the response of, "Okay, I'll play a game with you." Gray's special instructions explain exactly how to make up Comic Strip Conversations to help develop a theory of mind in any situation and for any age person.

## "Chill Out"

For teens and adults, Gray has created a tool called Thinking Stories. These stories help people to understand slang, idioms, figures of speech, and sayings that are often used in social situations. Gray says these stories "describe unstated meanings." She uses the example of "I'll catch you later."[28] It means, of course, seeing someone later or getting together with someone. People with AS, however, may take the statement literally and think the speaker is going to grab them or trap them at a later time. Other people with AS may know that the statement does not make literal sense, but they may be very confused about what it does mean. Examples of this kind of social speech are: "Has the cat got your tongue?" "You're pulling my leg," "Chill out," and "I've changed my mind." Teens and adults with AS can make lists of such language use and memorize their meanings. Friends, teachers, and families have to be ready to explain the real meaning and be tolerant of misunderstandings.

Since AS difficulties cannot be cured, often the treatment strategy is one of teaching other people to tolerate differences and helping people with AS to adapt and cope rather than to get over the problems. One of the ways that AS people learn to cope is with "rescue questions." These are the signals that tell other people that their social conversation is confusing. Attwood says that people with AS can be taught to say things like "I'm confused, can you please explain what you mean?" or "Are we understanding each other?"[29]

## Imitating Neurotypical Behavior

Another way to learn to participate acceptably in social situations is through drama classes. Teens with AS can enjoy drama classes in high school or college. They have a script to follow and a director to tell them what gestures to make and how to display emotions. They are practicing what to say and how to say it in typical situations. They can learn not to interrupt, how to chat, how to take turns in speaking with someone else, and how to give compliments or say friendly things. Most likely the script will avoid talking on and on about a special interest or being brutally honest about another person's faults. People with AS have a hard time learning the "little white lies" that neurotypical people use all the time. They do not say "I like

# Memorizing Social Rules

*From his practical experience with AS, teenager Luke Jackson suggests that other teens with AS memorize and carefully follow some basic advice he has learned for being socially acceptable. Because distinguishing between different social situations is so hard, people with AS do best when they just stick with certain rules all the time. Luke advises:*

- Don't "invade" people's space—that means get too close to them.

- Don't stare at someone for whatever reason.

- Don't make comments about people's bodies, good or bad.

- Don't tell dirty, sexist or racist jokes or make sexual innuendos.

- Don't hug or touch people unless they are part of your family or they have agreed to be your boyfriend or girlfriend and you have both agreed to do it.

Luke Jackson, *Freaks, Geeks, & Asperger Syndrome.* London and Philadelphia: Jessica Kingsley, 2002, pp. 104–5.

your new hairdo" if they think it is ugly. They do not know how to pretend interest in a topic. They do not know how to limit their talk about a special interest. Drama classes can teach these skills quite effectively. People are role-playing to learn social skills, and very often these skills can be imitated in real life.

Liane Holliday Willey, a woman with AS, recommends classes in drama, psychology, sociology, and speech for people with the disorder. She explains, "Somehow, I was able to dissect the nuances of human behavior far more effectively when I was a student studying it as a science than when I was an individual trying to figure it all out through experience and intuition."[30]

## Coping Tricks

Classes, logic, and imitation cannot solve all of the social difficulties involved in living with AS. One of the major problems—that of sensory overload and oversensitivity to stimulation—demands a different approach. The person may have trouble with certain sounds, visual stimulation, smells, touches, or tastes that is so extreme that the sensitivity interferes with everyday life. Little tricks can make a big difference. Earplugs and tinted glasses can help when sounds and sights are unbearable. Special tinted glasses developed by researcher Helen Irlen act as filters for many people with AS who wear them. Other people grow long hair that they can use as a subtle screen or curtain to protect them from strong lights. But often

A boy with autism wears a full-body sack that limits his exposure to sensory stimuli and makes him feel secure, an extreme example of tools and techniques that people with autism spectrum disorders use to manage their environments.

the tolerance and understanding of other people is necessary, too. In the classroom, for example, a student with AS may need to be assigned a desk away from bright sunlight. Teachers and friends may have to avoid hugging or suddenly and without warning touching a person with AS. They can also learn to accept that the student with AS cannot look them in the eye when they are talking.

Little children who cannot tolerate the textures of foods may be taught to gradually adjust by first licking the food and then holding it in the mouth without chewing. Parents can allow the child or teen with AS to choose his or her own clothing so that the texture is comfortable. They can cut out the tags if the tickling of the tag is unbearable. If certain places such as particular stores or theaters are too stimulating, the person with AS can be allowed to avoid those places or to leave any situation and find a quiet place when the stimulation is too much.

Understanding and tolerance are a form of therapy and treatment, too. They help people with AS feel comfortable, accepted, and capable of coping. Nita Jackson, a British woman with AS, describes the therapeutic behavior of one of her favorite teachers that helped her succeed in school and maintain her self-esteem:

> Mr. Osbourne was always bubbly and ready to make a light-hearted joke out of anything. He rarely got angry or raised his voice like most of my other teachers did. He let me hide in the music department's store cupboard at break time, without even blinking an eye, it was as though he understood and accepted why I needed to go to ridiculous measures to separate myself from society. I respected him for not probing for answers like everyone else did. Occasionally he would tap on the door, say "boo!" and offer me a biscuit [cookie] (which I never declined). On the last day of term, I bought him a tin of biscuits in return for the amount of biscuity yumminess he had allowed me.[31]

# Therapy or Fraud?

The Kennedy Krieger Institute in Baltimore, Maryland, estimates that there are more than three hundred treatments for autism spectrum disorders that have never been proved worthwhile. These so-called alternative treatments are usually tried by desperate parents who want to see their children cured of the disorder. One of the most popular treatments is chelation therapy. It is based on the idea that tiny amounts of metals from vaccines or foods have built up in and poisoned the body. Chelation therapy is a way of chemically removing these metals, using either pills or medicines given with a needle inserted in the arm. This treatment has never been scientifically tested, and the side effects of one of the drugs, DMSA, can be unpleasant or even dangerous. People have had rashes and vomiting. Animal studies have shown damage to the brain caused by DMSA. Another drug used in chelation therapy apparently killed one child in 2005.

Most scientists call chelation therapy for autism "voodoo medicine," but other researchers have asked for permission to do a scientific experiment with autistic children. They say many families have tried it, and its efficacy should be tested. In 2008 the National Institute of Mental Health considered funding the study. Some scientists said it would be unethical to subject children to dangerous chelation studies, so the funding is on hold until the safety concerns can be resolved.

## Not Everything Needs Changing

Treatment, toleration, and teaching are not the only ways to help people with AS. Perhaps the most important way that neurotypical people can intervene in the lives of people with AS is by respecting their differences and recognizing a real value in the Asperger way of thinking. Honesty, intelligence, logic, the ability to focus intensely on a topic, a unique way of experiencing the world—these are just a few of the talents that people with AS may possess. Attwood believes, for example, that special interests may have to be controlled if they interfere with getting along in society, but he does not believe they should be discouraged. Fascination with mathematics or computers, for instance, may lead to new inventions and creative developments in the future. He says that "it is important to consider not only the benefits to the person with Asperger's syndrome, but also the benefits to society."[32] He adds, "We need people with Asperger's syndrome to bring new perspective on the problems of tomorrow."[33] The best and most complete therapy for people with AS may be appreciation of their strengths, as well as helping them overcome their weaknesses.

# CHAPTER FIVE

# Living in an Alien World

Luke Jackson was twelve years old when he found out he had Asperger's syndrome. One day in his home in England, his mother casually plopped an article on the table in front of him. Luke, being an avid reader, picked it up and, for the first time in his life, discovered some important answers about himself. The article was about AS, and Luke realized that he had every symptom listed. He remembers: "It was as if I had a weight lifted off my shoulders. . . . I had finally found the reason why other people classed me as weird. It was not just because I was clumsy or stupid. . . . I finally knew why I felt different, why I felt as if I was a freak, why I didn't seem to fit in. Even better, it was not my fault!"[34]

## A "New and Improved Model"

Luke's mother had known he had AS since he was about seven years old, but she had been afraid to tell him and afraid he would feel bad about himself. Luke, however, was tremendously relieved. Knowing he had AS helped him to feel better about his behavior. It helped him to deal with living in the neurotypical world. Far from being stupid, Luke is a gifted teen who wrote an advice book for other AS teens when he was just thirteen years old. He titled it *Freaks, Geeks, & Asperger Syndrome*,

# Asperger's in History

When the diagnostic characteristics of Asperger's syndrome are applied to famous figures in history, a long list of people who may have had AS is available. The list includes scientists Albert Einstein (who could not speak fluently until he was seven years old) and Isaac Newton (who had to drop out of high school). Abraham Lincoln, Thomas Jefferson, and Napoléon Bonaparte may have had AS. Writers Jane Austen and George Orwell had AS traits. Composers Ludwig van Beethoven (who reportedly poured ice water over his head before he wrote music) and Wolfgang Mozart showed symptoms of AS. Peanuts creator Charles Schulz and Muppet inventor Jim Henson could have had AS. Today rock star Gary Numan and Pokémon inventor Satoshi Tajiri have been diagnosed with AS. Diagnosing people in history with Asperger's is controversial, but some researchers enjoy comparing AS traits to the descriptions of the behavior of famous people.

President Abraham Lincoln is one of many prominent individuals throughout history who modern researchers say demonstrated characteristics typical of people with Asperger's syndrome.

because even if he is a "freak," he does not care. He has learned to see himself as a "new and improved model"[35] of human being. Luke's struggle to see himself in a positive way is the hardest part of living with AS, but it is a journey that every person with AS has to make. As people with AS grow up, they have to adjust and adapt to the complex social demands of a larger world. Not all of their problems are unique to AS, but their ability to cope can be sorely tested. In the end, however, many are remarkably successful.

When children with AS are little, they often get along without too much trouble. If they want to talk about batteries or spark plugs, adults will listen indulgently. If they have tantrums when overstimulated, parents may not understand the real reason, but they do know tantrums are normal for young children. If AS children need to be alone, it is easy to escape to a bedroom where no one disturbs them. Even when families recognize that something is wrong, small children have little understanding that they are different. That all changes as children grow up and have to cope with the social world of school, making friends, and following teachers' rules.

## Being a Misfit

A teenager who posted his story anonymously on an AS Web site called O.A.S.I.S. was diagnosed at age twelve. He says that he had always known he did not fit in and was different. But the worst problems started around the fifth grade, before anyone knew he was struggling with AS. Around this time, he became terribly sad because of his social awkwardness and lack of friends. A doctor put him on medication for depression. Nevertheless, he describes trying to be socially normal at school as "draining, discouraging, angering, and depressing."[36] After this young man was diagnosed, he understood why he had trouble, but that did not prevent middle school and high school from being tough challenges. He was bright and had no problems with the academic work, but he remained an outsider—someone who was laughed at and teased for his differences.

Slowly the teen memorized "cool and timely sayings" and copied the social skills of others. He made so many mistakes,

Children and teens with Asperger's syndrome tend to be socially awkward, making it difficult for them to make friends and fit in with their peers.

however, that he was rejected and scorned by most of the other students. He was the last to be picked when others were choosing sides for a game. He did weird things such as doing his homework during recess instead of socializing. When people told jokes at his expense, he could not understand them. He says he was an "easy target"[37] for bullying.

As he progressed through high school, the teen eventually made a few close friends and learned to accept himself. His social problems improved. Today this courageous young man offers advice for others with AS. He says that AS is not a prison sentence but a description of one way of being, and he strongly believes that the AS way is legitimate and acceptable. He does not want to be changed. He offers this analogy:

Imagine placing a layer of peanut butter on top of a piece of bread, and then a layer of jelly on top of that, and then another layer of peanut butter. The layer of jelly is analogous to a person's Asperger Syndrome. An attempt to remove the layer of jelly smoothly would prove to be impossible, and if the jelly were removed, the piece of bread would be left looking completely different afterwards because a great amount, possibly all, of the peanut butter would have to removed as well. The sandwich may be more traditional without the jelly, and on some days, its eater may not be in the mood for the jelly, but acceptance of the jelly's presence can go a long way.[38]

# Explaining to the World

*Liane Holliday Willey does not mind telling anyone she has Asperger's syndrome, but sometimes she needs a quick and easy way to do it. For example, she often gets lost, feels confused, and needs to ask strangers for help. She finally printed up a business card that she could carry with her and hand to people. It reads, in part:*

I have Asperger's Syndrome, a neurobiological disorder that sometimes makes it difficult for me to speak and act calmly and rationally. If I have given you this card, it probably means I think I am acting in a way that might be disturbing to you. In short, Asperger's Syndrome can make it difficult for me to: speak slowly, refrain from interrupting, control my hand movements and my blinking. It also makes it hard for me to follow your thoughts so that I might misunderstand what you are trying to say or do. It would help me if you would speak calmly and answer any questions I might have, clearly and completely. I apologize if my behaviors seem inappropriate.

Liane Holliday Willey, *Pretending to Be Normal.* London and Philadelphia: Jessica Kingsley, 1999, p. 129.

# Bullying

Acceptance does not come easily for most school-aged people with AS. Teasing and bullying are common. Luke feels as if he has been bullied his whole life. He figures that some people just pick on anyone who is different. He is different in the way he is often alone at school instead of with friends and because he does not make an effort to fit in by acting tough and engaging in fights. Luke was never willing to fight; he says he does not "see the point." He also objects to "running with the pack" and acting interested in topics that bore him. He says, "I never have and I never will. I don't see any point in pretending that I like things when I don't." He adds, "This kind of stuff is beyond my comprehension. The one thing I have noticed in this life is that the world is full of idiots."[39]

Luke has a mature attitude and a determination to be true to himself, but that meant that he was punched, shoved, kicked,

Because of their behavioral differences and limited social defenses, young people with Asperger's syndrome can be an easy target for bullies.

laughed at, and called names. One day Luke tried to escape the bullying by hiding in the school changing rooms. The two worst bullies found him all alone. He says they

> began toying with me in much the same way as a cat plays with a mouse. Pulling and pushing, teasing and cajoling, they seemed to revel in my discomfort. Thinking of nothing but the need to escape these brainless baboons, I pushed my way past them and kept on running. Through the schoolyard, out of the school gates, I ran and ran but still they pursued me only to finally catch up with me and shower me with kicks and punches.[40]

A passing adult finally saw the torment and chased off the boys, but for Luke, it was the last straw. He and his mother decided it was time to change to a private school, and Luke never went back to that public school again.

Today Luke has learned strategies for avoiding being bullied. He knows better than to go off by himself when he is at school. He has taken tae kwon do, a martial art, for several years and learned to defend himself. Even though people with AS may do badly at team sports, they can do well with individual sports that do not demand social interaction. Luke says his coordination was terrible at first, but with the help of his teacher he got over his clumsiness and learned to love the physical training. One thing that Luke refuses to do, however, is try to change who he is. He is happy when by himself; he is devoted to his special interests; and he chooses his few friends carefully. He likes himself the way he is. He argues, "Why should we have to behave like everyone else just so that we don't get picked on? That is *so* unfair!"[41]

## Labeled and Judged

Tim Page, a man diagnosed with AS as an adult, would agree. He remembers failing in school because it was so hard to pay attention even though his intelligence was superior. He could make no friends among his classmates, who treated him like a freak. When his class was playing team sports, such as kickball or baseball, he felt continually humiliated. Teammates

teased and taunted him as he inevitably missed the ball altogether. He often ended up in tears while comforting himself
with all the things he could do. He did not understand why
other students thought his special interest in the history of
music and films was worthless. He gave up trying to be an accepted part of the group. "Meanwhile," he says, "the more
kindly homeroom teachers, knowing that I would be tor-
mented on the playground, permitted me to spend recess peri-
ods indoors, where I memorized vast portions of the 1961
edition of the *World Book Encyclopedia*."[42]

Page was not diagnosed with AS until 2000, when he had already become a successful music critic and writer, but the diagnosis was a relief. He finally had an explanation as to why
even his teachers and parents had disapproved of him. His
teachers were angry at his failing grades and his poor social
skills. His parents kept taking him to doctors and therapists to
find out what was wrong with him. His gym teacher treated
him with such contempt that he still says she is "the only person in the world I just might swerve to hit on a deserted road."[43]

Adults may not bully people who are different, but they
often misunderstand people with AS and treat them poorly.
John Elder Robison was not diagnosed until he was forty years
old, so he dealt with the misinterpretation of his behavior
throughout most of his life. When at last he understood his AS,
he felt extreme relief and finally realized, "I was not a heartless killer waiting to harvest my first victim. I was normal, for
what I am."[44] Robison never felt violent or cold and heartless,
but he had heard the accusation from family and teachers so
often as a child and teenager that he feared he was a secret
criminal inside. Because he could not bear to look into people's eyes and could not display his emotions, they said things
like "What are you hiding?" "You're up to something. I know
it," "You look like a criminal," and "I've read about people like
you. They have no expression because they have no feeling."[45]

Robison remembers: "I pondered it endlessly. I didn't attack
people. I didn't start fires. I didn't torture animals. I had no de-
sire to kill anyone. Yet. Maybe that would come later, though. I
spent a lot of time wondering whether I would end up in

prison."[46] Today Robison says, "In fact, I don't really understand why it's considered normal to stare at someone's eyeballs." He adds, "In fact, in recent years I have started to see that we Aspergians are *better* than normal!"[47]

## Misunderstood

Learning to accept oneself and feeling normal is not easy when adults act as if an AS teen is defective or bad. Luke remembers one class experience when he was daydreaming (which he knows was wrong), but the teacher's reaction and the communication mistakes that followed demonstrate just how difficult it can be to be an AS thinker in a neurotypical world:

> The angry teacher interrupted Luke's daydream and growled, "Jackson, would you care to tell us exactly where you are?"
>
> Luke (taking the question literally) replied, "Class E2, Sir."
>
> The angrier teacher responded, "Are you trying to be smart?"
>
> Luke (again literally) says, "Yes, sir." He knows everyone is supposed to try to be smart in school and assumes the teacher will be pleased with his answer.
>
> Furiously, the teacher exclaims, "Jackson, I will not, I repeat not, tolerate such insolence. You can pull your socks up or get to the headmaster [principal]."
>
> Luke smiles. He has finally learned that "pull your socks up" does not mean he is supposed to lean over and pull up his socks. He is proud that he understands this figure of speech. He grins to himself and picks up his pencil to get on with his work, as the teacher ordered him to do.
>
> The teacher is outraged by Luke's facial expression. He snarls, "This is no laughing matter and how dare you ignore me when I am speaking to you?"[48]

Luke is completely confused and ends up with detention that day. This is what it is like to live with AS, more often than not. Luke comments in his book that when he was younger, he might have had a tantrum over the unfairness, but now he has learned to control his temper. His trick is to think about his special interests to calm himself down.

## Enjoying an Asperger's Syndrome Life

Living with AS is not all negative experiences. Being alone and concentrating on special interests are sources of happiness for most AS people. Luke's special interests include computers, PlayStation, and Pokémon. He can spend many hours absorbed in computer games or just talking about the workings of computers. And he has found some friends who enjoy the same activities he does, even if they do not enjoy the same level of detail that he enjoys.

Stephen Shore, a man with Asperger's, remembers how meaningful his special interest was when he was young. He says:

> Catalogues and manuals were always of great interest and comfort as they were predictable. Often I compared sizes and versions of products offered in the catalogues. Air conditioner capacities as expressed in British thermal units caught my fancy one day, so in every catalogue I would seek the highest capacity air conditioner that ran on 115 volts alternating current.[49]

Many experts believe that special interests are a source of comfort and predictability in an otherwise confusing, chaotic world. Special interests can help people with AS to be less anxious, to feel calm and comfortable, and to find pleasure in an environment where other people can be rejecting and unfriendly. One woman with AS explains, "It's easy to bestow love onto objects rather than people because although they can't love back they can't rebuke either." She adds that a special interest provides a safe place "where no one can get hurt."[50] Nita Jackson, a teen with AS, found pleasure in a collection of Barbie dolls and My Little Ponies. She did not play with the dolls and ponies. She lined them up and organized them by their names in alphabetical order. Only as she grew older was she able to extend her interests to people.

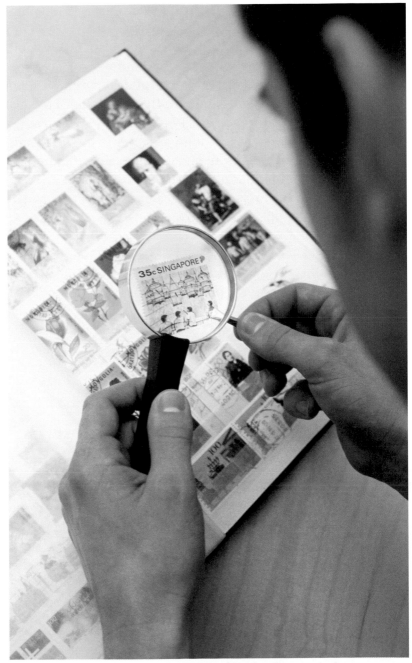

People with Asperger's syndrome tend to develop special interests in games, collections, or other activities that bring them pleasure and satisfaction.

Liane Holliday Willey continues to find pleasure and comfort in one of her special interests. She says that most of her AS traits have "faded away" as she has matured, but she still needs a way to relax. One of her special interests is architecture. She says, "To this day, architectural design remains one of my most favorite subjects and now that I am older I indulge my interest, giving in to the joy it brings me."[51] Willey adds, "When I feel blighted by too many pragmatic mistakes and missed communications, I find my home design software programs and set about building a perfect sense home. There is something about the architectural design process that makes my brain click and fit."[52]

## Special Interests for Lifelong Satisfaction

Temple Grandin, a woman with either high-functioning autism or AS, had a special interest in animals throughout her childhood. She was able to feel compassion for animals and to understand their feelings in a way she never could manage with people. When she grew up, her special interest became her career. She is a professor at Colorado State University and an expert on animal behavior and caring for livestock. She says she is living proof that people with autism spectrum disorders can live happy, successful, and fulfilled lives, despite their differences.

Grandin's lifestyle may not be typical. She does not have a lot of close friends, for example, but she is satisfied with her limited social contacts. She once explained:

> I know that things are missing in my life, but I have an exciting career that occupies my every waking hour. Keeping myself busy keeps my mind off what I may be missing. Sometimes parents and professionals worry too much about the social life of an adult with autism. I make social contacts via my work. If a person develops her talents, she will have contacts with people who share her interests.[53]

Grandin's life and the lives of people with AS may be different, but many have come to realize that they can celebrate that difference and be glad to be the people they were meant to be.

# CHAPTER SIX

# A Bright Future

The first children diagnosed with Asperger's syndrome during the 1990s are now teens and young adults. They and the people diagnosed in adulthood continue to contribute to the body of scientific knowledge about AS. Much more needs to be learned, not only about diagnosing and treating AS, but also about how best to help people with AS to live full and meaningful lives. Many research studies are being conducted today so that scientists can gather more information and solve the mysteries of the disorder. The long-term goals of these studies include finding better diagnostic tools, identifying the causes of AS with certainty, and discovering which treatment methods and therapies are most effective. Often, people with AS have another goal for the future: They want to persuade the world to make room for the AS way of being.

## Earlier Identification

Accurate diagnosis of AS is still difficult, and most children do not get a diagnosis until after the age of five. Attwood explains that a diagnosis "cannot yet be made with sufficient confidence in pre-school children."[54] Some children with AS are not diagnosed until they are twelve or older. Researchers and therapists say that this is too late. They point out that the earlier

AS is diagnosed, the sooner treatment can start and the sooner social skills can be learned. Perhaps, they say, fewer children would have severe AS symptoms if this could be done. Early diagnosis would also mean that a child would have less chance of becoming depressed, frustrated, or anxious because he or she is different and criticized. It could mean that the child learns to understand and accept being the kind of person he or she was born to be. It might mean that the adults in the child's life no longer treat that child as defective or disturbed.

Diagnosis is difficult, however, because there is still disagreement about the early signs of AS. One long-term study is trying to identify behavior in babies that may indicate an autism spectrum disorder. The study is supported by the National Institute of Mental Health and is being conducted by Sally J. Ozonoff at the University of California at Davis and Marian Sigman of the University of California at Los Angeles. The researchers are following the growth and development of infants who have a brother or sister already diagnosed with an autism spectrum disorder. Because autism runs in families, they expect that a percentage of the babies will develop an autism spectrum disorder themselves. The scientists will keep careful records of the behaviors and development of all the babies. They will compare the early characteristics of those who become autistic with those who do not and look for the traits that might be the diagnostic tools of the future.

## More Accurate Diagnosis

Behavior in very young children with autism spectrum disorders, however, can appear perfectly normal, so researchers are also looking for the genes and brain differences that could lead to early, reliable diagnosis. The Autism Genetic Resource Exchange (AGRE) is the world's first "gene bank for autism."[55] Families can enroll in the AGRE program if they have more than one member diagnosed with an autism spectrum disorder. The program takes blood samples from the family members and stores frozen DNA samples in its bank. Parents or other adults are interviewed, videotaped, and audiotaped, and the results are also saved. Children may be videotaped so that their behaviors are on record for further study.

Because autism runs in families, researchers are studying the infant siblings of children diagnosed with autism spectrum disorder in order to identify autistic traits demonstrated by infants and toddlers and thus allow for earlier diagnosis.

So far, out of about 1,000 families, 345 have had a complete genetic map stored in the AGRE data banks. Any autism researcher can use the AGRE gene data in his or her own study of the genetics of the disorder. The future goal of AGRE is to have thousands of data samples available so that autism researchers can use the large amount of information to identify the genetic and biological markers of autism. Someday, AGRE researchers hope to have a genetic blueprint of autism that can be used to diagnose autism spectrum disorders and perhaps even point the way to a cure.

In England the Autism Research Centre at the University of Cambridge is conducting a gene study of people with AS by comparing their DNA with the DNA of a brother or sister. If the researchers are successful at finding meaningful DNA differences between siblings, they may discover important information about diagnosing and treating AS. In an effort to distinguish between high-functioning autism and AS, scientists at McLean Hospital in

Test tubes at a human gene bank contain specific samples of DNA. Researchers have created a gene bank focused on the collection of DNA from people with autism spectrum disorder and their families in hopes of furthering understanding of the genetics behind the condition.

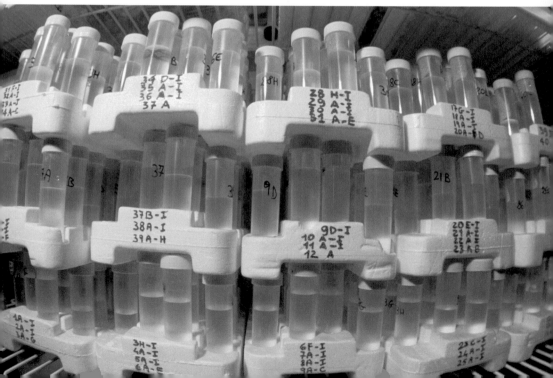

Massachusetts, Yale University, the University of Michigan, and the University of Chicago are collecting DNA samples and brain images of people diagnosed with both disorders. They also will look for differences that may lead to better diagnoses someday.

## Genes Plus Environment?

Many researchers wonder, however, whether genes are the only cause of AS. Some suspect that the genes may set up a vulnerability to AS but that environmental factors actually trigger the disorder, or at least make it more severe. Researchers think one of these factors might be problems with digesting certain foods, which could lead to allergies affecting the normal growth of the brain. Food sensitivities might cause chemical changes in the brain that could be corrected with the right medications.

At the University of Delaware, researchers are conducting surveys of people with AS to look for connections between diet and AS symptoms. The survey consists of questions, usually answered by a parent, about foods. Some of the questions are:

- Does your child have any food allergies?

- Do types of foods seem to affect your child's behavior?

- Does your child have . . . stomach or gastrointestinal troubles?[56]

This study is just a beginning in the search for the possible effects of diet on AS. There is very little scientific evidence that foods and allergies can affect autism spectrum disorders, but many people believe there is a connection. Luke, for instance, is on a special program to eliminate gluten (in wheat flour and other grains) and casein (primarily in milk and dairy products) from his diet. He says about his diet, "It has made a massive difference to my life and the lives of many others and if it doesn't help, then no harm has been done."[57] Luke Jackson believes that he has overcome stomach problems, diarrhea, bad breath, and rashes by eliminating gluten and casein from his diet. He also thinks it has helped his AS symptoms to get better. He sleeps better than he used to, can concentrate better, and is more in control of his emotions.

Some researchers and parents contend that children with autism spectrum disorders improved when they eliminated gluten (found in wheat products such as bread) and casein (found in dairy products such as milk) from their diets.

The diet Luke follows was developed by pharmacist Paul Shattock at the University of Sunderland in Great Britain. His theory is that people with autism spectrum disorders do not use, or metabolize, gluten and casein properly, perhaps because of their genes. These food proteins then cause poisons or toxins to build up in the body that affect the brain in negative ways. The trouble with this theory is that almost no scientific studies have been successful in proving it. Scientists who have tried to test the theory with careful studies have not yet found a connection between autism and diet. Nevertheless, thousands of people claim the diet has helped them or their children. Researchers say that many more studies are necessary in the future to determine if a special diet such as this one can reduce the symptoms of autism spectrum disorders. The University of Delaware survey asks parents about special diets and any results they have noticed. The survey is an initial effort to at least collect reports of the benefits of gluten-free and casein-free diets.

## Better Medical Treatments

Other researchers are looking for medicines and drugs that may help people with autism spectrum disorders to function more normally. Many people with AS take Ritalin, a drug for overactivity that can help them concentrate and focus on learning. Others may take drugs that treat depression or anxiety. These drugs are common, but in recent years, many children and teens have been prescribed other drugs in the hopes that they will ease some AS symptoms. Risperdal, for example, is an antipsychotic usually prescribed for people with serious mental illness. It is given to young people with AS not because they have a mental illness, but because it sometimes helps them to control frustration and tantrums.

The problem with this kind of drug use, however, is that most of the medicines have not been tested on children and teens. In 2000 the National Institute of Mental Health decided that information on the safety and effectiveness of such drugs had to be determined. It helped to establish the Pediatric Pharmacology Research Units Network at several universities in different cities. The network continues to conduct trials and

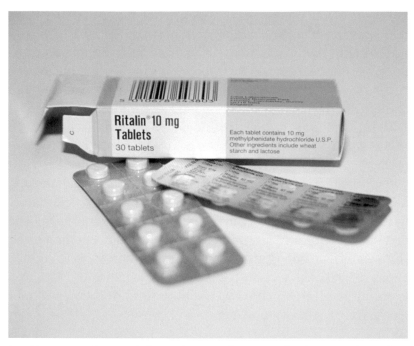

Ritalin is one of several drugs that may be prescribed to people with autism spectrum disorders.

studies of drugs commonly given to young people for autism spectrum disorders. In the future the National Institute of Mental Health hopes that clinicians will know if they are making good decisions with prescriptions and will be able to make the best choices for people with AS.

## A Future Without Asperger's Syndrome?

Researchers and clinicians are studying the effects of different kinds of drugs that they hope will ease the symptoms of AS and perhaps make AS brains function more like neurotypical brains. So much research is going on and so much is being learned that many people think a medical cure for autism spectrum disorders is going to be possible. Not everyone, however, is pleased with this idea. Many people with high-functioning autism and AS find the search for a cure to be discriminatory and just plain wrong. Luke, for instance, says, "This is a really controversial subject because lots of people (including me) think that looking for a cure for autism can be likened to Hitler trying to create an Aryan race."[58] Luke's statement may sound extreme, but his point is that people with differences should be appreciated and accepted, not erased from the population. He understands that people with severe autistic symptoms— trapped in a world of their own and unable to communicate— need help and even a cure. But he does not want such a cure for himself. Most people with AS agree with him.

Asperger himself wondered if the disorder represents a kind of genius and theorized that autistic people have been responsible for untold creative improvements and inventions throughout history. He said: "It seems that for success in science or art, a dash of autism is essential. For success, the necessary ingredient may be an ability to turn away from the everyday world, from the simply practical, an ability to rethink a subject with originality so as to create new untrodden ways, with all abilities canalized [channeled and focused] into the

# Voted Out of Kindergarten

In the spring of 2008, five-year-old Alex Barton was voted out of his kindergarten class by his classmates by a majority of 14 to 2. The vote was Alex's teacher's idea. Prompted by the teacher, the kindergarten children labeled Alex's behavior in class as "disgusting" and "annoying." The teacher thought Alex was undisciplined and disruptive. She was trying to teach him that actions like crawling under a table and kicking it were bothering the whole class. She told him to listen to what the other children did not like about him. Alex has AS, and his experience is not the kind of future that AS activists want for children like him. They hope that every child with any disorder can enjoy an education that makes room for his or her differences. They want every child to feel special and understood.

Quoted in Asperger Square 8, "Not Special: Support Alex Barton," May 24, 2008. http://aspergersquare8.blogspot.com/2008/05/not-special-support-alex-barton.html.

one specialty."[59] More recently, Temple Grandin, who has been responsible for inventions herself, said, "If the world was left to you socialites, we would still be in caves talking to each other."[60] Her point is that logical and unsocial ways of thinking and working have helped civilizations to evolve. Perhaps the world desperately needs people with AS.

Thomas, an eleven-year-old boy with AS, has a creative way of expressing this idea. His mother reports that he was reading a book about AS when he said, "Mom, in this book, they talk about Asperger's disorder. Why do they refer to Asperger's as a disorder?" His mother replied that it was a good question and she did not know. Thomas continued, "I'm going to write the author of this book and tell her she used an incorrect term. Actually, I'm not in disorder. I am definitely in order."[61]

## Aspie Pride

Aspies for Freedom (AFF) is an activist group of people with Asperger's syndrome that says that being an "aspie" is a source of pride. The group rejects the idea that being on the autism spectrum is a disease and argues that it is not always a disability. The AFF Web site declares:

> We know that autism is not a disease, and we oppose any attempts to "cure" someone of an autism spectrum condition, or any attempts to make them "normal" against their will. We are part of building the autism culture. We aim to strengthen autism rights, oppose all forms of discrimination against aspies and auties [autistics], and work to bring the community together.[62]

This may seem like a surprising statement, but AFF members have very different goals for the future than most researchers and clinicians do. They oppose many current treatments. They do not want society's pity and do not want to be cured. Their goal is to see a change in the way people with AS are treated by society and to be supported in their efforts to fit into the neurotypical world. They say, "Many problems associated with autism are caused, or worsened, by prejudice." They want to persuade society to have a "positive and realistic

Some advocates seek to promote the acceptance of people with Asperger's syndrome by emphasizing an appreciation for their creative gifts, accommodation for their learning needs, and acceptance of their differences.

idea"[63] of what it means to be on the autism spectrum. They believe, for example, that schools that insist that people with AS should adjust to noisy environments are prejudiced. They believe that people should be able to be employed whether or not they like to socialize with neurotypicals in the workplace. They say demanding "normal" social skills is prejudice. Activist groups such as Aspies for Freedom believe that the best and happiest future will be one in which people with AS are not expected to act like neurotypical people and are valued for their creative ways of thinking.

## Aspies and Neurotypicals Together

GRASP, another AS support group, believes the best future is one in which people with autism spectrum disorders help each other to succeed in the neurotypical world. GRASP stands for the Global and Regional Asperger Syndrome Partnership. It is an advocacy group, run by people with AS and autism, that provides educational and support services for all people on the autism spectrum. The GRASP mission includes recognizing that members have a responsibility to themselves and to society as a whole, increasing public awareness about autism spectrum disorders, teaching themselves how to get along in their communities, and improving the lives of people with AS and autism. It also aims to describe the positive aspects of AS, as well as its negatives. Positive characteristics of AS, according to GRASP, include honesty, lack of hypocrisy, loyalty, trusting personality, passion about a topic or interest area, orderliness, excellent memory, independent thinking, and great powers of concentration.

One of the ways that GRASP wants to make a difference is to change the terms used to describe AS people. The changes will help raise self-esteem and pride for people with AS. They will also help neurotypical people to abandon their prejudices against those on the autism spectrum. The GRASP Web site urges that "normal versus abnormal" is a negative wording for neurological differences. It states that the appropriate term is not *normal* but *neurotypical*. It says that *disorder* is a prejudicial term, while *condition* or *diagnosis* is a better one. It labels *disease* a bad term and *syndrome* a good term. It asserts that *cure* is a wrong term that should be replaced with *understand*.[64]

Michael John Carley, the founder and executive director of GRASP, is a man with AS who also has a son with the syndrome. He believes that learning to get along in the neurotypical world, or conforming, has its place. He says that people can assimilate, or act as neurotypical as possible, if they wish. But he also believes that AS people should be allowed not to conform and not to assimilate. He explains, "GRASP fights very hard for people's right not to have to conform, for such pressure can often be society's attempts to subconsciously demonize or denounce so-called

# A Wish for the Future

*Dawn Prince-Hughes is a doctor of anthropology and an expert on gorilla behavior. She also has AS, but she was not diagnosed until adulthood. Her childhood and youth were painfully difficult as she struggled with people who did not accept her nor offer any ways to help her cope. She knows she has achieved success now, but she does not want other children to suffer the experiences she did. She explains:*

> I will always grieve for the small child and the young woman running away from the light, the noise, the taunts, the fists, my racing mind. Those scars don't heal and I don't want them to. I have been carved like a stone and that's what it has taken. I hold a hope, sweetly, that other children can become all they can be—something different than what I am now—by having a kinder experience.

Quoted in Random House of Canada, "Author Interview." www.randomhouse.ca/catalog/display.pperl?isbn=9781400082155&view=auqa.

Anthropology professor Dawn Prince-Hughes's memoir, *Songs of the Gorilla Nation: My Journey Through Autism*, traces her experience living with Asperger's syndrome.

autistic behaviors. But so too should no one criticize the choice of someone on the spectrum to advance in the world through assimilation. . . . We must instead respect each other's choices."[65]

Today's adults with AS grew up undiagnosed and misunderstood. Their adjustment to the neurotypical world was fraught with pain and difficulty. The members of GRASP want to see a different kind of future for today's AS children and teens. Carley believes that they will achieve bright futures by becoming self-aware and being comfortable with who they are. He says, "[We] want to be creating in kids the best self-advocates they possibly can be because we hope that they're going to leave home, and they need to be the ones to explain why they come across as different to that potential landlord, significant other, or employer."[66] At the same time, say O.A.S.I.S. leaders, "Everyone with Asperger syndrome should be respected and celebrated for their differences."[67]

# Notes

## Introduction: Strangers in a Foreign Land

1. Damian, interview with the author, Dundas, VA, July 18, 2008.
2. Damian, interview.

## Chapter 1: What Is Asperger's Syndrome?

3. Tony Attwood, *The Complete Guide to Asperger's Syndrome*. London and Philadelphia: Jessica Kingsley, 2007, p. 208.
4. Quoted in Attwood, *The Complete Guide to Asperger's Syndrome*, p. 209.
5. Patricia Romanowski Bashe and Barbara L. Kirby, *The OASIS Guide to Asperger Syndrome*. New York: Crown, 2001, p. 43.
6. Attwood, *The Complete Guide to Asperger's Syndrome*, p. 216.
7. Quoted in The National Autistic Society, "Asperger Syndrome: What Is It?" www.nas.org.uk/nas/jsp/polopoly.jsp?d=212.
8. Quoted in Bashe and Kirby, *The OASIS Guide to Asperger Syndrome*, p. 27.
9. Quoted in Attwood, *The Complete Guide to Asperger's Syndrome*, p. 272.
10. Michael John Carley, *Asperger's from the Inside Out*. New York: Perigee, 2008, p. 18.

## Chapter 2: Diagnosing Asperger's Syndrome

11. Attwood, *The Complete Guide to Asperger's Syndrome*, pp. 50–52.
12. Quoted in Barbara L. Kirby, "What Is Asperger's Syndrome?" O.A.S.I.S. www.udel.edu/bkirby/asperger.

13. James Robert Brasic, "Pervasive Developmental Disorder: Asperger Syndrome," eMedicine, March 11, 2008. www.emedicine.com/ped/TOPIC147.HTM.

14. Christopher Gillberg, Carina Gillberg, Maria Rastam, and Elisabet Wentz, "The Asperger Syndrome (and High-Functioning Autism) Diagnostic Interview (ASDI): A Preliminary Study of a New Structured Clinical Interview," *Autism* 2001, pp. 64–65. http://aut.sagepub.com.

15. Attwood, *The Complete Guide to Asperger's Syndrome*, p. 53.

16. Susan Dickerson Mayes, Susan L. Calhoun, and Dana L. Crites, "Does DSM-IV Asperger's Disorder Exist?" *Journal of Abnormal Child Psychology*, June 2001. http://findarticles.com/p/articles/mi_m0902/is_3_29/ai_76558499?tag= untagged.

17. Attwood, *The Complete Guide to Asperger's Syndrome*, p. 46.

## Chapter 3: Born Different: What Causes Asperger's Syndrome?

18. Attwood, *The Complete Guide to Asperger's Syndrome*, p. 327.

19. Quoted in PhysOrg.com, "UCLA Study First to Show Autistic Brains Can Be Trained to Recognize Visual and Vocal Cues," June 22, 2007. www.physorg.com/news101739453.html.

20. Cornelis Bakker, Russell Gardner Jr., Vassilis Koliatsos, Jacob Kerbeshian, John Guy Looney, Beverly Sutton, Alan Swann, et al., "The Social Brain: A Unifying Foundation for Psychiatry," *Academic Psychiatry*, September 2002. http://ap.psychiatryonline.org/cgi/content/full/26/3/219.

21. Attwood, *The Complete Guide to Asperger's Syndrome*, p. 112.

22. Attwood, *The Complete Guide to Asperger's Syndrome*, p. 114.

23. Peter Szatmari, "Unravelling the Mystery of Autism: An Interview with Dr. Peter Szatmari," Offord Centre for Child Studies. www.offordcentre.com/asd/asd_art4.html.

24. Attwood, *The Complete Guide to Asperger's Syndrome*, p. 345.

## Chapter 4: Treatments and Therapies for Asperger's Syndrome

25. Attwood, *The Complete Guide to Asperger's Syndrome*, p. 156.
26. Ofer Golan and Simon Baron-Cohen, "Systematizing Empathy: Teaching Adults with Asperger Syndrome or High-Functioning Autism to Recognize Complex Emotions Using Interactive Multimedia," Abstract, *Development and Psychopathology*, 2006, Cambridge Journals, March 28, 2006. http://journals.cambridge.org/action/displayAbstract?from Page=online&aid=420155.
27. Quoted in O.A.S.I.S., "Social Stories and Comic Book Conversations." www.udel.edu/bkirby/asperger/socialcarolgray. html.
28. Carol Gray, "Thinking Stories: Social Stories™ That Describe Unstated Meanings," The Gray Center. www.thegray center.org/cms/ktmlliterf/files/uploads/Thinking%20Stories.pdf.
29. Attwood, *The Complete Guide to Asperger's Syndrome*, pp. 212–13.
30. Liane Holliday Willey, *Pretending to Be Normal*. London and Philadelphia: Jessica Kingsley, 1999, p. 132.
31. Quoted in Attwood, *The Complete Guide to Asperger's Syndrome*, p. 247.
32. Attwood, *The Complete Guide to Asperger's Syndrome*, p. 201.
33. Attwood, *The Complete Guide to Asperger's Syndrome*, p. 255.

## Chapter 5: Living in an Alien World

34. Luke Jackson, *Freaks, Geeks & Asperger Syndrome*. London and Philadelphia: Jessica Kingsley, 2002, p. 34.
35. Jackson, *Freaks, Geeks & Asperger Syndrome*, p. 35.
36. Quoted in O.A.S.I.S. Kids' Corner, "Asperger Syndrome Experiences from a Teenage Perspective." www.udel.edu /bkirby/asperger/teens_reflection.html.

37. Quoted in O.A.S.I.S. Kids' Corner, "Asperger Syndrome Experiences from a Teenage Perspective."

38. Quoted in O.A.S.I.S. Kids' Corner, "Asperger Syndrome Experiences from a Teenage Perspective."

39. Jackson, *Freaks, Geeks & Asperger Syndrome*, pp. 143–45.

40. Jackson, *Freaks, Geeks & Asperger Syndrome*, p. 137.

41. Jackson, *Freaks, Geeks & Asperger Syndrome*, p. 150.

42. Tim Page, "Parallel Play," *New Yorker*, August 20, 2007. www.newyorker.com/reporting/2007/08/20/070820fa_fact_page.

43. Page, "Parallel Play."

44. John Elder Robison, *Look Me in the Eye*. New York: Crown, 2007, p. 238.

45. Robison, *Look Me in the Eye*, 2007, p. 2.

46. Robison, *Look Me in the Eye*, pp. 2–3.

47. Robison, *Look Me in the Eye*, p. 240.

48. Jackson, *Freaks, Geeks & Asperger Syndrome*, pp. 103–4.

49. Quoted in Attwood, *The Complete Guide to Asperger's Syndrome*, p. 176.

50. Quoted in Attwood, *The Complete Guide to Asperger's Syndrome*, p. 175.

51. Willey, *Pretending to Be Normal*, p. 77.

52. Willey, *Pretending to Be Normal*, p. 58.

53. Quoted in Attwood, *The Complete Guide to Asperger's Syndrome*, p. 344.

## Chapter 6: A Bright Future

54. Attwood, *The Complete Guide to Asperger's Syndrome*, p. 54.

55. AGRE Home Page. www.agre.org.

56. University of Delaware Center for Disabilities Studies, "Autism Diet and Nutrition Survey." www.udel.edu/bkirby/asperger/importantnews.html.

57. Jackson, *Freaks, Geeks & Asperger Syndrome*, p. 83.

58. Jackson, *Freaks, Geeks & Asperger Syndrome*, p. 77.

59. Quoted in Attwood, *The Complete Guide to Asperger's Syndrome*, p. 332.

60. Quoted in Attwood, *The Complete Guide to Asperger's Syndrome*, p. 332.

61. Quoted in Attwood, *The Complete Guide to Asperger's Syndrome*, p. 334.
62. Aspies for Freedom Home Page. www.aspiesforfreedom. com/index.php.
63. Aspies for Freedom Home Page.
64. GRASP, "About GRASP: Beliefs." www.grasp.org/ab_beliefs. htm.
65. Carley, *Asperger's from the Inside Out*, p. 158.
66. Quoted in Johanna Sorrentino, "Understanding Asperger's Syndrome," *Education.com*, March 29, 2008. www.grasp. org/media/education.com.pdf.
67. Bashe and Kirby, *The OASIS Guide to Asperger Syndrome*, p. 471.

# Glossary

**amygdala:** A part of the brain that helps to regulate emotions and acts as a first warning system by sending chemical signals to other parts of the brain.

**autism:** A brain disorder that impairs social relationships, interactions, and communication and is characterized by a seeming withdrawal from the world and a turning inward to restricted behaviors and interests.

**autism spectrum disorder:** A term for the range of disorders that includes autism and Asperger's syndrome and refers to the combination and range of autistic characteristics that can vary from mild to severe.

**chromosomes:** Structures in the nuclei of cells that carry hereditary information in the genes.

**clinicians:** Professionals such as psychiatrists, psychologists, and medical doctors who are involved in treatment, therapy, and diagnosis and are directly involved with patients and clients.

**deoxyribonucleic acid (DNA):** The chemicals in the genes that carry the coding instructions for all body structures and functions.

**empathy:** The ability to identify with and understand the emotions and physical feelings of another person as if they were one's own.

**fight or flight response:** The biological and neurological reaction to danger. The body automatically gets ready to either fight or run away when the animal or person senses a frightening or stressful situation.

**functional magnetic resonance imaging (fMRI):** A medical technique that can identify which parts of the brain are active by the amount of blood flow that is detected.

**genes:** Discrete segments of DNA, on specific points of a chromosome, that carry specific units of inheritance.

**high-functioning autism:** An autism condition in which communication is possible, intelligence is normal or high, and the individual's social impairments are not severe.

**magnetic resonance imaging (MRI):** A medical test that uses a large magnet, radio waves, and a computer to produce detailed pictures of body structures.

**mind blindness:** An inability to develop an awareness of what another person is thinking or feeling because of an inability to read the social clues. It is the opposite of empathy.

**mind reading:** Using one's empathy to predict or understand another person's behavior.

**neurological:** Involving the nervous system and the brain.

**neurotypical:** A term for people with typical neurological development and behavior.

**self-stimulation:** Behavior that seems to have the purpose of activating or stimulating the senses and may be a way of focusing or shutting out unwanted stimulation.

**sensory:** Relating to the senses, such as vision, hearing, smell, taste, and touch.

**special interest:** A topic or activity that preoccupies and fascinates people with Asperger's syndrome.

**stereotyped:** Defining behaviors that are repeated many times and seem meaningless, such as rocking or head banging.

**theory of mind:** The ability to empathize with other people so that one can make sense of their reactions and behavior. This makes it possible to recognize thoughts, feelings, intentions, and beliefs in other people.

# Organizations to Contact

**Asperger Syndrome Coalition of the United States**
2020 Pennsylvania Ave. NW, PO Box 771
Washington, DC 20006
phone: (866) 427-7747

This nonprofit organization is dedicated to providing up-to-date information and advice for and about people with high-functioning autism, Asperger's syndrome, and related disorders.

**Autism Information Center, CDC**
1600 Clifton Rd.
Atlanta, GA 30333
phone: (800) 232-4636
e-mail: cdcinfo@cdc.gov
Web site: www.cdc.gov/ncbddd/autism

The U.S. Department of Health and Human Service's Centers for Disease Control and Prevention provide extensive information about autism spectrum disorders, downloadable fact sheets, and general publications. It also conducts and funds research into all aspects of autism spectrum disorders.

**The Autism Society of America**
7910 Woodmont Ave., Ste. 650
Bethesda, MD 20814
phone: (800) 328-8476

The Autism Society's goals are to improve the lives of people with autism and to raise public awareness about the needs of people with an autism spectrum disorder. It is a leading source of information about autism and other spectrum conditions. Advisers to the society include autistic people themselves.

**Autism Speaks**
2 Park Ave., 11th Fl.
New York, NY 10016
phone: (212) 252-8584
e-mail: contactus@autismspeaks.org
Web site: www.autismspeaks.org

Autism Speaks is an activist organization that funds research into the causes, treatments, and possible ways to cure autism.

**GRASP**
666 Broadway, Ste. 830
New York, NY 10012
phone: (888) 474-7277
Web site: www.grasp.org

This is the national headquarters of GRASP, the Global and Regional Asperger Syndrome Partnership. The organization is run by and for people on the autism spectrum and will help people with Asperger's or autism to find information, locate support groups, and  set up a GRASP chapter of their own.

# For Further Reading

## Books

Carrie Fredericks, *Autism*. Detroit: Greenhaven, 2007. With an anthology of articles by experts in the field, this book explores what autism is, the controversies surrounding the causes and treatments of autism, and how Asperger's syndrome differs from classic autism.

Kathy Hoopmann, *All Cats Have Asperger Syndrome*. London and Philadelphia: Jessica Kingsley, 2006. This lighthearted and funny book is an introduction to AS via photos and simple descriptions of aloof, cute, and independent cat behavior.

Luke Jackson, *Freaks, Geeks & Asperger Syndrome*. London and Philadelphia: Jessica Kingsley, 2002. This book of advice for teens with Asperger's syndrome was written by thirteen-year-old Luke Jackson. With humor and insight, he covers such topics as special interests, bullying, and learning social language. Expert Tony Attwood says the book is informative and educational for anyone who wants to understand Asperger's syndrome.

Jessica Peers, *Asparagus Dreams*. London and Philadelphia: Jessica Kingsley, 2003. Jessica, a twelve-year-old diagnosed with Asperger's syndrome, was sent to a private school for children with autism. In this autobiography she describes the difficulties she faced and the emotional problems she had to overcome while living in a British institution.

Jude Welton, *Can I Tell You About Asperger Syndrome? A Guide for Friends and Family*. London and Philadelphia: Jessica Kingsley, 2004. The author is the mother of a child with Asperger's syndrome who explains the disorder in her own child as well as how it affects kids in general. She emphasizes the good qualities of people with AS and helps friends and family to understand the unique AS way of thinking.

## Web Sites

**Kids' Corner: Contributions from Our Kids, O.A.S.I.S.** (www.udel.edu/bkirby/asperger). At the home page of the O.A.S.I.S. Web site, scroll down the menu on the left and click the link to the Kids' Corner. The page contains links to stories, poems, and art created by young people with Asperger's syndrome.

**LukeJ369 Design** (www.lukejackson.info/index2.html). Luke Jackson, now nineteen years old, is busy turning his special interests into a career. To see what he is up to, as well as read about his other activities and an update on his life, visit his newly designed Web site.

**Neuroscience for Kids—Asperger's Syndrome** (http://faculty. washington.edu/chudler/asp.html). Read about the brain and Asperger's syndrome and see illustrations of the brain lobes. Click the links for "autism" and "frontal and parietal lobes" to learn more.

**Tony Attwood** (www.tonyattwood.com.au/index.html). At Tony Attwood's official Web site, visitors can read information about Asperger's syndrome, find out the latest news about AS, and learn something about the background of this foremost expert on Asperger's syndrome.

**What's Your AQ? Pie Palace** (www.piepalace.ca/blog /asperger-test-aq-test). Just for fun (*remember, no one test is diagnostic*), visitors to this blog can take an Asperger's syndrome questionnaire designed by Simon Baron-Cohen and check out their Asperger's quotient.

**Wrong Planet.net** (www.wrongplanet.net). This Web site is one of the largest online communities for people with autism spectrum disorders.

# Index

# Picture Credits

# About the Author

Toney Allman holds a B.S. from Ohio State University and an M.A. in clinical psychology from the University of Hawaii. She currently lives in Virginia and has written more than thirty nonfiction books for students on a variety of topics. She is grateful to all the people with Asperger's syndrome who have so generously written and spoken about their life experiences.